The Librarian's Complete Guide
to Involving Parents
Through Children's Literature

The Librarian's Complete Guide to Involving Parents Through Children's Literature

Grades K-6

Anthony D. Fredericks

Illustrated by
Phyllis Disher Fredericks

1997
Libraries Unlimited, Inc.
Englewood, Colorado

To Debby Mattil—warm friend, valued colleague, and marketing manager extraordinaire.

LIBRARIES UNLIMITED, INC.
P.O. Box 6633
Englewood, CO 80155-6633
1-800-237-6124
www.lu.com

Production Editor: Kevin W. Perizzolo
Copy Editor: Jason Cook
Proofreader: Susie Sigman
Indexer: Linda Running Bentley
Typesetter: Kay Minnis

Library of Congress Cataloging-in-Publication Data

Fredericks, Anthony D.
    The librarian's complete guide to involving parents through children's literature : grades K-6 / Anthony D. Fredericks.
        xxi, 137 p. 22x28 cm.
        Includes bibliographical references (p. 107) and index.
        ISBN 1-56308-538-0
        1. Children--United States--Books and reading. 2. Reading--Parent participation--United States. 3. Children's literature--Problems, exercises, etc. 4. Activity programs in education.
Z1037.A1F775   1997
028.5'344--dc21   97-256
                                                                            CIP

Contents

Books and Activities

Acknowledgments

I am forever indebted to the scores of children's librarians, public school librarians, and children's literature experts around the country who shared with me their enormous knowledge of children's books in the preparation of this book. I am fortunate to have been influenced by such a marvelous cadre of individuals from north and south and east and west. In particular, I salute the following:

To Paula Gilbert, who consistently earns the title "World's Greatest Children's Librarian," goes a thousand tips of the hat for wisdom shared and friendship treasured.

To Peggy Sharp, whose knowledge of children's literature is exceeded only by her skill in sharing her love of books with others, goes my absolute and unconditional appreciation.

To Jan Kristo, a fellow "partner in crime" in both professional and social endeavors, go my undying love and steadfast respect.

To Liz Rothlein, a colleague who epitomizes the "best of the best" in this grand and glorious profession, goes my sincerest admiration for her continuous contributions and unwavering support.

To Suzanne Barchers, a gifted editor and esteemed friend, goes a thunderous standing ovation (and lots of giant hugs).

And to all the kids in all the storytelling programs around the country who never stopped telling me, "Please. Please, read it again." Well . . . let's do it!

Introduction

"Wow!"

"That was really neat!"

"Read it again!"

"Read it again. Please. Please read it again!"

What librarians have long known intuitively and what has been validated with a significant body of research is the fact that the stories, books, and literature shared between parents and children have wide-ranging and long-lasting implications for the educational and social development of children. That is to say, when parents share stories with their children, they are providing youngsters with windows into long-ago times, faraway lands, and make-believe places. Parents are sharing the magic of possibilities that expand the world and "energize" imagination as no other activity can. The simple act of reading a book to, or creating a story for, a child becomes a positive and significant event in the development of that child.

Though the magic of sharing good books and imaginative stories has always been the centerpiece of the work of school and public librarians, and an objective fiercely promoted to the parents of the children with whom they work, it is equally true that many librarians around the country are engaged in another concern in communities large and small. Tight financial budgets and shrinking resources for both community and school libraries are placing enormous burdens on libraries in terms of services offered, hours open, and availability of personnel. Too many libraries have had to reduce their offerings to the schools or public simply because of a lack of funds. In far too many cases, staff reductions have left many libraries with "skeleton crews," or with no crews at all. It is an unfortunate fact that community and school librarians are frequently the first to be let go when budgets are tightened and finances trimmed. Readers are well aware of the effect of these decisions on the children and citizens of the community.

That librarians are battling an army of financial dragons while dodging the swords of staff cutbacks and skirting the cannon fire of reduced hours makes their jobs even harder. What remains constant, however, is an unfailing desire to broaden their base of appeal, to reach out to a larger and larger clientele, and to promote the worthiness of their institution as a viable component in both school and local communities. In short, many librarians have become not only promoters of good literature, but promoters of their place in the lives of their clientele, both young and old.

In discussions with public and school librarians around the country, it became clear that "public relations" efforts aimed at "recruiting" parents as allies, friends, and supporters of the library have resulted in a broadened base of support and a solidarity of patronage that frequently ensures the continuance of library services. In other words, when parents are invited to take an active role in the promotion of good books and good reading habits for their children, they provide a supportive structure that can safeguard the viability and longevity of a library. So, too, are librarians assured that their services are both well received and necessary to the educational and social milieu of both school and community.

This book is designed to help you reach out and enjoin parents as partners in your literary efforts. It is also designed to expand and extend the library's services and cement your role as a vital community resource. Its success will depend on how eagerly it is embraced and how actively it is promoted as an essential element in the literature you share with youngsters.

The projects, activities, and suggestions offered in this book do not rely on the accumulation of bodies of knowledge, nor do they require parents to have skills other than a love for, and understanding of, their youngsters. The intent of these activities is to encourage strong bonds of communication between parents and children, not to create the ideal shoe box diorama or perfect salt map for display in the library. In short, the products are of less importance than the processes used to create those products. Feel free to suggest alternate strategies or modifications of these ideas. Helping parents take advantage of natural learning situations will be more important than asking them to complete "assignments" that are time consuming or with which they are uncomfortable. Invite parents (and their children) to suggest additional activities or other possibilities for selected books. In so doing, you will be providing them with a sense of ownership and additional opportunities to promote reading as a lifelong process.

Providing opportunities for parents to assume an active role in the promotion of good children's literature can be accomplished in many ways. Parents need to understand that their involvement in any literature outreach program must be for the direct benefit of their children. Or conversely, parents must know that they are not engaged in some "busy work" project designed by the librarian. What is most important is that parents understand that outreach efforts are a vital part of the library's services and a necessary element to the growth of literacy in children. As a librarian, you can assume a pro-active role in the promotion of your institution's services while broadening its influence in the larger community.

It is my sincere hope that you will discover a plethora of possibilities to expand and extend your literacy efforts into the homes of your clients. In so doing, you will promote a heightened sense of enjoyment, achievement, and participation for all children. Additionally, you will be helping to cement the "literature bond" that can take place between parents and children—a bond that can promote a lifelong love of reading and an enduring sense of appreciation for the library.

How to Use This Book

This book is designed to help librarians build a lasting and enthusiastic relationship with parents and to help parents extend the learning opportunities of their children through a literate environment. Encouraging parents to become supporters of their children's literacy growth and development can be one of your most important tasks.

Book Selection

There are hundreds of thousands of children's books available for youngsters, and more than 5,000 new children's books are published each year. No book of this size could begin to address all the available literature. Selections for this book were based on a combination of the following consultations and considerations:

1. Selected books include those recommended as the most appropriate children's literature, for a variety of reading abilities, by children's librarians in public schools and public libraries. Books checked out of school and public libraries in many parts of the country, as well as librarians' personal choices, were considered.

2. Selected books include those recommended by teachers and reading specialists as engendering positive responses from students and providing opportunities for parents and children to share the reading experience through cooperative activities. Also consulted were annual editions of "Teachers' Choices"—an annotated list of new children's trade books for children and adolescents that teachers throughout the country find to be exceptional. (Single copies of each year's "Teachers' Choices" list are available free. Write to: International Reading Association, 800 Barksdale Road, P.O. Box 8139, Newark, DE 19714-8139. Enclose a self-addressed 9-by-12-inch envelope stamped with first-class postage for two ounces.)

3. Selected books include children's choices. Several editions of "Children's Choices"— an annual compilation of favorite books as designated by school children throughout the United States—were consulted. (Single copies of each year's "Children's Choices" list are available free. Write to: International Reading Association, 800 Barksdale Road, P.O. Box 8139, Newark, DE 19714-8139. Enclose a self-addressed 9-by-12-inch envelope with first-class postage for four ounces.) Also consulted were editions of "Young Adults' Choices"—an annual collection of popular books as determined by students in middle, junior, and high schools throughout the United States. (Single copies of each year's "Young Adults' Choices" list are available free. Write to: International Reading Association, 800 Barksdale Road, P.O. Box 8139, Newark, DE 19714-8139. Enclose a self-addressed 9-by-12-inch envelope with first-class postage for two ounces.)

4. Selected books include award-winning children's literature—Caldecott Medal and honor award books, Newbery Medal and honor award books, Children's Book Award books, American Library Association Notable Books for Children, Reading Rainbow Feature books, and Boston Globe/Horn Book Award winners.

5. Selected books represent a cross-section of high-quality children's literature that includes different genres (fantasy, science fiction, historical fiction, informational, biographies, etc.) and literary elements (theme, plot, point of view, characterization, and setting).

6. Selected books extend and enhance children's language development. Through a selection of the "classics" and contemporary titles, children can examine and explore the world around them as well as engage in meaningful language-rich experiences with their parents.

7. Selected books are easily accessible by parents in any school or public library. The literature selection includes books that could be part of family libraries.

8. Selected books are entertaining and enjoyable. Some books will be familiar to children; some will not. The overall intent is that children receive a balanced exposure to books that will serve as a foundation for a lifetime of reading pleasure.

The appendix consists of four lists of recommended children's literature, each containing more than 90 suggested children's books for specific grade levels. These lists may be duplicated and given to parents. These books meet the same criteria for the 101 books selected for the body of this work.

Important Features

This book has several features of particular interest to the school or public librarian:

1. This book contains activity pages for 101 children's literature selections. These pages are designed to be duplicated on one sheet of paper to be sent home with children as part of a regular or special library program (e.g., a summer reading program). The activity page for each book contains:

    a. Bibliographic information (title, author, publisher).

    b. A brief summary of the book.

    c. Discussion questions that parents and children can share after the book has been read or during the reading of the story. The intent is not necessarily to have parents ask all of the questions, but rather to stimulate parent-child discussion.

    d. Activities that parents and children can do together. These extensions of the book are appropriate to a wide range of abilities and interests of children.

    e. A list of related titles for children and parents to enjoy together. These include books on the same theme and books written by the same author.

2. There is no prescribed sequence for the literature selections. You should feel free to distribute the pages in whatever order you wish. Most librarians will probably elect to send them home in random order, although it is possible to coordinate certain literature selections with particular elements of the local school's reading and language arts curriculum. The literature selections are arranged alphabetically, not by reading level.

3. You are encouraged to use as many (or as few) of the activity pages in this book as you deem appropriate. You may elect to use them throughout an entire school year, within the context of a special program or outreach effort, or during a specific library event (e.g., "Spring into Reading").

4. Each activity page is designed to offer parents and children a variety of relaxing, non-threatening, and supportive activities that extend the book and encourage families to

participate actively in the discussion and sharing of good literature. While it is certainly important for parents to read to their children on a regular basis, it is equally important that parents and children have sufficient opportunities to discuss books and work together in learning activities that bring literature to life and make books an important part of all children's lives. Thus, there are no tests to give, no "checking up" to do, and no grades to assign. These activity pages are designed not as homework assignments but rather as extensions of the library program. There is no obligation for you to follow through on whether each family has completed a requisite number of activities for each book. Busy schedules and hectic weeks may preclude some families from doing the suggested activities for a particular book. That's O.K.! Parents should not feel any obligation to read any particular book and do the accompanying activities during the week that the activity page is sent home. You might suggest that parents obtain a three-ring binder in which they can keep activity pages for future reference and use. In this way, families will be able to share a specific book and its accompanying activities at a time that is most convenient to them.

There are many ways to distribute these activity pages. You should choose those approaches most appropriate to the dynamics of your library and community:

1. Duplicate each activity page on single sheets of paper. Send them home with children once a week or once every other week on a specific day of the week. You may wish to designate one day of the week (Fridays or Tuesdays, for example) as literature activity page days. By selecting a specific day of the week, parents will come to expect the activity page and may be able to plan for extended periods of time to pursue the designated activities with their children.

2. Discuss the selected book with children before distributing the activity page. Introduce the author and illustrator, provide an appropriate overview of the plot and theme, and suggest activities that children can do with their parents. If convenient, you may wish to designate a specific day of the week or month as a "Summary Day"—a day for sharing some of the activities children did with their parents to extend specific books and some of the things children discussed with their parents.

3. Add your own suggestions to activity pages. This will allow you to personalize an activity page according to the specific needs of an individual child. This sends a signal to parents that you are willing to do more than simply photocopy an activity page for them; rather, you are interested in providing them with ideas that are tailored specifically for their child.

4. Send the "Introductory Letter" (see p. xxi) to parents before initiating any of the subsequent activity pages. This letter will provide parents with valuable information on the dynamics of your program and the role they are expected to play. You may want to mail the activity pages instead of sending them home with children.

5. Consider sending the activity pages in packets. Although these pages can be sent home on a weekly or biweekly basis, you may want, for example, to send home two activity pages every two weeks or four pages every month. Such an option allows you and parents more opportunities to introduce books, and children more opportunities to read books independently and pursue suggested activities in depth.

6. It is not important that all children receive the same activity pages at the same time (this may cause a "run" on the library for a specific book). You may want to create a rotating schedule for giving out activity pages throughout the year. This will ensure better access to selected literature. It might be advantageous to duplicate as many of the pages as possible and have them on hand to send home randomly throughout the year.

7. Because many schools send home a periodic newsletter to parents, you may want to attach the activity pages to the school's newsletter. In so doing, you will be expanding the effectiveness of the literature program for more parents.

8. Consider calling parents to ask if they are receiving the activity pages. Ask how they are enjoying sharing activities with their children. This will provide you with an opportunity to recommend other books and activities for parents and their children.

9. Ask a member of the local community (e.g., elementary principal, superintendent, mayor, council-person, etc.) to write a letter to parents that mentions the importance of these activity pages and the reasons why parents and children should share the books and the extending activities.

10. Make sure that any special functions at school (e.g., "Meet the Teacher Night," open houses, book fairs, parent/teacher conferences) include information on these activity pages. Samples of the activity pages and descriptive information can be easily distributed to all parents or to parents of children in specific grade levels during these school functions. Any special function or event at the public library should also include the distribution of these activity pages.

11. Encourage children to suggest alternate ways for distributing these activity pages to parents. They may wish to consider some of the following methods of distribution:

    a. Record activities on cassette tape, make copies, and distribute to parents.

    b. Distribute the activity pages through a local community agency (e.g., YMCA, Boy's Club, Little League, day camps, etc.).

    c. Distribute the activity pages through a fraternal organization (e.g., Moose, Elks, Rotary, Knights of Columbus, etc.).

    d. Distribute copies in bulk to community buildings (e.g., town hall, community meeting rooms, etc.).

    e. Include portions of an activity page in newsletters distributed by local clubs, organizations, or religious groups.

    f. Post samples of activity pages on community bulletin boards.

12. Promote the activity pages and their usefulness in various communications with parents. Phone calls, meetings, conferences, and notes can all be vehicles for disseminating information.

The success of these activity pages as well as the success of your parent and community outreach efforts will depend upon constant communication and regular "public relations" with parents. These activity pages and the literature they promote can be viable elements in all your promotional ventures.

Promoting the Literature Bond

You may wish to consider the following list of suggestions for promoting literature to families and promoting literature bonds between parents and children. It is vitally important that you maintain a regular system of promotion efforts throughout the year. This alerts parents to the notion that books and literature should be a vital part of not only the school and public libraries, but also the "home curriculum."

- Set up special literature workshops for parents. Monthly meetings can present new children's books and the accompanying activities and projects parents and children can do together to extend literature in the home.

- Prepare public service announcements on the value of parents and children reading books together. Distribute these to local radio stations.

- Prepare stories or messages to be placed on the library's telephone answering machine, including a selected book and one or two accompanying activities.

- Prepare special brochures, flyers, or leaflets on selected children's books (children might wish to help). Send these to parents periodically.

- Write a "letter to the editor" of a local newspaper on the value of parents and children reading together. Offer a bibliography of selected children's books for interested readers.

- Invite parents to visit your library on a regular basis to read selected books to a group of children.

- Hold a monthly "Parent Tea" to share ideas and discuss new books added to the public or school library.

- Ask the district superintendent (school library) or head librarian (public library) to prepare a letter to send to parents on the value of reading in the home.

- Set up a "telephone tree"—a system by which parents can call other parents to relay news about children's books and suggested activities for these books.

- Invite parents to participate on a "Literature Council" to help select new books for the public or school library.

- Call several parents each week to share information about children's books.

- Have children write form letters to families in your community or school. These letters could suggest popular or new books for families to share together as well as children's ideas for "hands-on" activities.

- Invite parents to participate in a "Family Reading Night," an evening in which parents and children gather to share favorite stories and selected extending activities.

- Have children design contemporary cards for selected books. The front of each card might have an illustration from a particular book along with bibliographic information. The inside of each card might suggest one or two extending activities for family use. Prepare and mail these cards to families throughout the year.

- Obtain approval to include a note about new children's books or popular children's literature with report cards.

- Send personal invitations to parents to bring a "brown bag lunch" and spend an afternoon at the library. This time can be used to share selected books individually and in small groups.

- Create a "Book of the Week" or "Author of the Month" program and disseminate information to parents in the form of a monthly newsletter.

- Schedule a series of home visits to meet with families. Take along a selection of relevant children's literature and share these books with parents.

- Invite children to prepare a series of posters "advertising" popular books. Distribute these posters around town (e.g., banks, post offices, stores, etc.). Replace the posters on a monthly basis.

- Provide opportunities for parents and children to work together on selected literature-based activities. With several libraries, coordinate a monthly meeting of parents and children throughout the community.

- Provide parents with a list of bookstores or teacher supply stores in your local area (some parents may not know where they can purchase children's literature).

- Establish a series of "make-and-take" workshops in which parents can create learning materials related to selected children's books. Distribute these materials to other parents in the community.

- Talk with parents about appropriate children's books during parent/teacher conferences. Prepare a list of suggested books for distribution at the conferences.

- Establish a "Parent Responsibility" contract. Design this contract to encourage a regular and specific amount of reading time for parents to spend with their children (e.g., 15 minutes each day).

- Keep aware of upcoming television shows and movies (many are based on children's books). Check a video store for movie versions of children's books and provide a list of these to parents (watching a video version of a book may encourage the reading of the original).

- Interview various groups of children about some of their favorite books. Prepare a list of these books and distribute it to families.

- Create a "Family Book of the Month" club and provide opportunities for families to share the books and stories they read at home. Send a monthly newsletter to families.

- Invite the town mayor to issue a "Families Reading Together" proclamation (a simple request on letterhead is often all that is needed).

- Invite children to design a parent involvement or literature logo that can be used on all outgoing messages and newsletters.

- Create an informal "quiz show" for families (e.g., "Literature Family Feud") about their knowledge of selected children's books.

- Invite children to send a letter or note to the parents of another child about why the parents should read a particular book with their child. Have children do this monthly.

- Prepare a list of recommended books to give to the parents of new students transferring into the community. A collection of activity pages from this book would also be an appropriate welcome for new students.

- Establish a "Grandparent's Club" in which grandparents and other senior citizens visit your library to share favorite children's books. Take photographs and have children conduct interviews and write reports for inclusion in a monthly newsletter or the local newspaper.

- Set up an exhibit in a local shopping mall including photographs of parents and children reading together, tips on parent participation, lists of recommended books for selected grade levels, and lists of home reading activities.

- Work with a group of children and parents to develop a slide show, including recorded narration of suggested children's books. Make the slide show available through the normal checkout system.

- Work with a local college's education department to create special parent programs on the use of children's literature in the home and the value of parents and youngsters reading together.

- Read a portion of a children's book to children. Encourage parents to obtain the book and complete the reading of the story at home.

- Prepare a series of brief notes that can be duplicated and attached to homework papers throughout the school year. Each page of notes should contain one or two recommendations for children's books and selected discussion questions and extending activities.

- Periodically, write letters to selected parents on recommended books for their children. Be aware of children's interests and suggest appropriate literature.

- Work with children to design a series of special certificates or awards to be sent to parents periodically. Give awards in recognition of parents sharing good literature with their children (however, awards should not be given for completing a specified number of activities).

- Prepare a checklist of things parents should do with their children at home to promote good books and good reading habits (appropriate samples can be found in *Letters to Parents* by Anthony D. Fredericks and Elaine P. LeBlanc [Glenview, IL: Scott, Foresman, 1986]).

- Invite children to set up a "Recruiting Office." Solicit ideas and suggestions from children on how to involve all families in a family reading program. What activities could children suggest that might encourage parents and children to share more books? Collect their ideas and distribute them through a newsletter.

- Establish a series of "Saturday Morning Book Talks." Each regularly scheduled book talk should introduce parents to new children's literature as well as extending activities families can share at home.

- Prepare videotapes of current books and selected activities to be used with the books. Make these videos available to parents.

As you use this book, please feel free to modify or alter activities and suggestions in keeping with the abilities of the children and the dynamics of your community. Ask parents how they are using these activity pages and how the pages can be improved. Providing opportunities for parents to "buy into" these activities will give them a sense of ownership that will result in heightened levels of participation. These activities achieve their greatest effect when parents know that their insights and feedback are valued. You will find these insights useful in future years.

These materials should help you communicate with parents about good books and good reading habits. Parent participation in the affairs of the school or public library can solidify the library's place as an important and significant feature of any community. When librarians and parents are actively engaged in a coordinated literacy effort, anything is possible.

Introductory Letter

Dear Parent or Guardian:

One of the questions parents frequently ask is, "What are some appropriate books for my child to read?" As you may imagine, when children are encouraged to read good literature and are supported in those efforts, reading skills develop dramatically. As part of our effort to help you help your child experience good books, we will be sending you specially prepared activity pages. Each activity page identifies a specific children's book recommended for your child. Included will be a brief summary of the book, discussion questions for you and your child to share, a selection of activities for you and your child to do together, and a list of additional children's books that you and your child might enjoy.

Each time you receive one of the activity pages, please obtain a copy of the recommended book. You can check out the book at the public library or the school library, borrow the book from a friend or neighbor, purchase a copy at a bookstore, or obtain a copy from your home library. Plan to read the book with your child over the course of several days. You may elect to read the book aloud to your child, your child may want to read the book by himself or herself, or your child may want to read the book aloud to you. It is important that you plan reading time each day with your child.

Upon completion of the book, share some of the discussion questions with your child. These questions are designed to help your child think critically about the book and what it means to him or her, not to "test" your child on what he or she remembers about the book. Of course, you and your child are encouraged to think of other questions to discuss, too.

Each activity page contains a variety of extending activities related to the book. It is not important that you complete all the activities. Share the suggestions with your child and choose together one or more you would enjoy doing. Each activity is designed to help your child gain a fuller appreciation of the book and to provide exciting learning opportunities. Most of the activity materials can be found at home or inexpensively purchased at craft and hobby stores, variety stores, department stores, and supermarkets.

The time you spend with your child reading these books and doing the suggested activities should be relaxed, comfortable, and supportive. By working together with your child in an encouraging way, you will be helping your child discover the wonder and excitement of good literature while also promoting his or her reading development. Reading the suggested books and participating in the suggested activities on a regular basis can be an important part of your child's growth in reading.

I'm looking forward to working with you. I hope you'll feel free to contact me at any time if I can provide you with any additional information or assistance.

Sincerely,

Books and Activities

1

Alexander and the Terrible, Horrible, No Good, Very Bad Day

Judith Viorst
New York: Macmillan, 1972

Story Summary

One day Alexander wakes up with gum in his hair. From the start, the entire day is filled with one misfortune after another. Alexander wants to move to Australia, but he realizes terrible days happen everywhere, even there.

Discussion Questions

1. If you were Alexander, what would you have done to change the day?

2. Could any of the other characters have helped Alexander to have a good day?

3. Does everybody have bad days? Why?

4. Is Alexander's day similar to a day you have experienced? How did you deal with your bad day?

Activities (Please select one or more activities.)

1. With your child, visit a library and obtain materials and resources on Australia (ask the Reference Librarian). Work with your child to create a descriptive brochure (sheets of paper stapled together) on the climate, animals, culture, and geography of Australia. What makes Australia unique?

2. Ask your child to write a brief essay about a recent bad day. What happened? How did your child feel? Have your child share the essay with other family members: Did they experience the bad day in the same way?

3. Ask your child to write an alternate version of the book, entitled *Alexander and the Wonderful, Terrific, Super, Fantastic Day*. Your child may want to record the story on a tape recorder or write it for other family members to enjoy.

4. Ask your child to pretend to be an advice columnist who can suggest strategies or solutions for Alexander to consider in dealing with his bad day.

5. Have your child interview an adult (parent, baby-sitter, neighbor, etc.) about the worst day he or she has ever experienced. Make sure your child takes notes during the interview. Have your child share the interview with the rest of the family.

Related Children's Books

Alexander Who Used to Be Rich Last Sunday by Judith Viorst
I Should Have Stayed in Bed by Joan M. Lexau
I Won't Go to Bed by Harriet Ziefert
It Could Always Be Worse by Margot Zemach

Max in Australia by Adam Whitmore
The Quarreling Book by Charlotte Zolotow
Sam's All Wrong Day by Gyo Fujikawa
Today Was a Terrible Day by Patricia Reilly Giff

2

Amazing Grace
Mary Hoffman
New York: Dial, 1991

Story Summary

Grace has a vivid imagination and loves to act out stories. However, when she wants to play the part of Peter Pan in a school play, Grace is told that she cannot because she is a girl and because she is black. Grace's mother and grandmother show her that she can be anything she wants to be. Eventually, Grace wins the part of Peter Pan and a stronger belief in her own abilities.

Discussion Questions

1. Are there any characters in this book who are similar to people in your family? Explain.
2. How was Grace able to overcome the "obstacles" in her life?
3. What did you enjoy most about the character Grace?
4. If you were to tell your friends about this book, what would you share?

Activities (Please select one or more activities.)

1. Invite your child to obtain a copy of *Peter Pan* from the school or public library. Plan a specific time to share the book with your child. Discuss with your child the similarities between Peter Pan and Grace.
2. Invite your child to begin a list entitled "Amazing Me"—personality traits that make him or her special. Periodically discuss with your child the items on that list.
3. Encourage your child to make a list of all the characters Grace liked to play (i.e., Joan of Arc, Anansa, Mowgli, etc.). Encourage your child to select one of these characters and to act out one or more scenes from that storybook character's life.
4. Talk with your child about a time when he or she was discouraged from doing something because he or she lacked a particular trait or skill. How did that event affect your child? What did he or she do about it? What could be done in the future?

Related Children's Books

Frederick by Leo Lionni
I Like Me by Nancy Carlson
I'm the Best! by Marjorie Sharmat
Much Bigger Than Martin by Steven Kellogg
On the Day You Were Born by Debra Frasier
The Pain and the Great One by Judy Blume
Ramona the Brave by Beverly Cleary
Today Was a Terrible Day by Patricia Reilly Giff

3

Blueberries for Sal

Robert McCloskey
New York: Viking, 1948

Story Summary

Sal and her mother go out to pick blueberries. Sal wanders to the other side of the hill, where she meets a baby bear. The baby bear ends up following Sal's mother, and Sal ends up with the mother bear. Eventually, the two youngsters find their own mothers.

Discussion Questions

1. How did Sal feel when she met the mother bear?

2. If you could change part of the story, which part would you change, and how?

3. Who is your favorite character in the story, and why?

4. What might have happened if Sal had not found her mother and baby bear had not found his mother?

Activities (Please select one or more activities.)

1. Have your child change the ending of the story, telling what would have happened if Mother Bear had taken Sal home and Sal's mother had taken Little Bear home. Your child may want to illustrate the new story and share it with a family member.

2. Purchase or gather a variety of berries (e.g., blueberry, red raspberry, black raspberry, blackberry, strawberry, gooseberry). Ask your child to taste the various berries and to describe the flavor, feel, size, and other characteristics of each type of berry. Later, you and your child may want to write and design a simple guide to different kinds of berries found in your area or local grocery store.

3. Take your child on a "bear hunt" throughout your house. Keep a log of all the different types of bears found. Some possibilities include: gummy bears, teddy bears, a bear T-shirt, bear books, bear-shaped cookies, bears in cartoons, bear note cards, a bear rubber stamp, and so on. Create a living room display of bears and bear paraphernalia, and keep a running log of all bear items found in the house.

4. With your child, brainstorm a list of the qualities of a real bear and, in a separate list, the qualities of a stuffed toy bear. Ask your child to note similarities and differences. Which type of bear does your child favor? Why? Which type would your child rather have in his or her bedroom?

Related Children's Books

Jamberry by Bruce Degen
My Mother Is Lost by Bernice Myers
One Morning in Maine by Robert McCloskey
Strawberry by Jennifer Coldrey

Box Turtle at Long Pond

William T. George
New York: Greenwillow, 1989

Story Summary

This is the story of an incredible journey—a day in the life of a box turtle. The turtle awakens, searches for food, finds shelter during a rainstorm, and comes into contact with other animals throughout the day (including an attacking raccoon). At the end of the day, the turtle finds shelter in tall grasses. This wonderfully illustrated book is a marvelous introduction to pond life and the daily cycle of a single organism.

Discussion Questions

1. What do you think was the most interesting part of the turtle's day?

2. Why did the author describe pond life through the "adventures" of a box turtle?

3. Did you learn anything new about pond life while reading this book? Explain.

4. What are some other "adventures" the turtle might have in succeeding days?

Activities (Please select one or more activities.)

1. Visit a pet store and obtain a small turtle as a pet for your child. Be sure to obtain instructions for proper care and feeding from the store personnel. Invite your child to keep a diary or journal of the turtle's activities over a period of several days. How do the activities of the pet turtle compare to those of the turtle in the book?

2. The turtle in the book ate some wild grapes. Take your child to a supermarket and purchase several varieties of grapes. What are the differences and similarities among the varieties (taste, size, shape, etc.)?

3. Take your child on a field trip to a nearby pond to observe the different plants and animals indigenous to the area. Your child may want to take photographs of various organisms or make sketches of selected plants and animals. Discuss any similarities between the organisms seen at the pond and those illustrated in the book.

4. Invite your child to keep a journal about the daily life of another animal (e.g., the family pet). Encourage your child to record any behaviors, travels, and "adventures" of the animal over a 24-hour period. What behaviors might be repeated in succeeding days? What did the animal do that was unusual?

Related Children's Books

And Still the Turtle Watched by
Sheila MacGill-Callahan
Fishing at Long Pond by William T. George
Look Out for Turtles! by Melvin Berger
The Moon of the Alligator by
Jean Craighead George

One Small Square: Pond by Donald M. Silver
Saving Our Wetlands and Their Wildlife
by Karen Liptak
Spoonbill Swamp by Brenda Guiberson
Wetlands by Pamela Hickman

5

Bridge to Terabithia

Katherine Paterson
New York: Harper & Row, 1977

Story Summary

Jess and Leslie become friends and establish a secret meeting place deep in the woods, where they create an imaginary kingdom called Terabithia. Their friendship comes to an end when Leslie falls and drowns in the swollen stream that must be crossed to reach Terabithia. Jess builds a bridge across the stream, as a lasting token of their friendship.

Discussion Questions

1. What qualities do you look for in a friend?

2. How do you feel about keeping secrets from your parents?

3. Is it important to have friends of the opposite sex? Why?

4. Why did Jess build a bridge across the stream?

5. If you could choose one of the story characters as your friend, who would you choose, and why?

Activities (Please select one or more activities.)

1. Using butcher paper or a large sheet of blank newsprint, have your child make a life-size cutout of his or her best friend: Draw and color the physical features of the friend. Cut a "door" into the chest area to view a list of inner qualities that make the friend special. (Write the qualities on a separate piece of paper, cut slightly larger than the door, and glue or tape the paper behind the door.) Your child may want to put the cutout friend in a special location.

2. After Leslie's death, Jess needed time to learn how to cope with his feelings. Several characters in the story helped him with this process. With your child, identify these characters and discuss how they helped Jess. Write the ideas on "helping hands"—hand-shaped cutouts. For example: Jess's father listened to his fears and held him close; Mrs. Myers shared her feelings about her husband's death; Bill gave Jess a puppy to care for; the puppy slept on Jess's chest and kept him company.

3. Leslie and Jess pretend that they are the rulers of a magic kingdom. Have your child write a short story about a kingdom he or she would like to rule.

4. Share the book *The Accident* by Carol Carrick (New York: Houghton Mifflin, 1976) with your child. Compare the events of this story to the events involved in the accidental death of Leslie. Discuss accidents with your child, noting that although many accidents are preventable, one does not always have control of a situation, and accidents will happen.

Related Children's Books

Death Is Natural by Laurence Pringle
Goodbye, Max by Holly Keller
The Kid's Book About Death and Dying
    by Eric Rofes
Learning to Say Goodbye by Eda LeShan

My Secret Hiding Place by Rose Greydanus
The Tenth Good Thing About Barney
    by Judith Viorst
When People Die by Joanne E. Bernstein

6

Bringing the Rain to Kapiti Plain

Verna Aardema
New York: Dial, 1981

Story Summary

This story involves Ki-pat, a herdsman who watches his cows go hungry and thirsty because there is no rain to make the grass grow. He watches a large cloud overhead and devises an ingenious way to make the rain come using a special arrow and a special feather.

Discussion Questions

1. How did the illustrations help you appreciate this story?
2. If you had an opportunity to talk with Ki-pat, what would you say?
3. Are the climatic conditions in this part of Africa similar to any conditions in the United States?
4. What did you enjoy most about this book?

Activities (Please select one or more activities.)

1. Read the story aloud to your child. Afterwards, invite your child to "read" along with you. Read the book again and pause at the beginning of each of the repeated phrases. Invite your child to "fill in the blanks" with words remembered from the story.

2. Have your child create a "folktale" using your town as the setting. Encourage your child to use the rhythmic pattern in the book. Following is an example that children can modify according to their locale:

> These are the great Pennsylvania hills,
> Sprinkled with farms and streams and mills—
> An ocean of trees for birds to soar through,
> And waves of flowers for insects to fly to.

3. Invite your child to watch as you fill an empty mayonnaise jar with boiling water. Allow the jar to sit for several minutes and then pour out about one-half of the water. Place the lid of the jar upside down on top of the jar. Put several ice cubes on the lid. Tell your child to watch for drops of water forming on the underside of the lid. Invite your child to speculate on the similarity between this activity and the formation of rain in the atmosphere. (Warm air holds more moisture than cold air. When moisture-laden air is cooled, as in the demonstration above, it loses that moisture and "rains.")

Related Children's Books

A Rainy Day by Sandra Markle
Listen to the Rain by Bill Martin Jr. and
   John Archambault
Rain: Causes and Effects by Philip Steele

Rain Talk by Mary Serfozo
That Sky, That Rain by Carol Otto
Thunder Cake by Patricia Polacco

7

Brown Bear, Brown Bear, What Do You See?

Bill Martin Jr.
New York: Holt, 1967

Story Summary

Using familiar animals, this book guides the reader through nine different colors in a rhythmic and enjoyable pattern.

Discussion Questions

1. Where are some other places you have seen these colors?
2. What are some colors that the author did not discuss? Where would they be found?
3. Is there such a thing as a blue horse? A purple cat? Why?
4. Are goldfish really made of gold?
5. What are some other colors for bears, frogs, birds, dogs, cats, horses, ducks, fish, and sheep?

Activities (Please select one or more activities.)

1. Give your child three disposable drinking cups, each filled with a primary color (red, yellow, and blue) of water-based paint, a small paintbrush, a paper towel, an old shirt (for drips), a cup of clean water, and a sheet of white construction paper. Invite your child to experiment mixing the colors to get new colors.

2. Help your child assemble an animal scrapbook. Cut out pictures of animals from old magazines and glue them onto sheets of construction paper. Staple or sew together the sheets of construction paper (along one side) to create a book. Your child may want to create several scrapbooks: land animals, sea animals, flying animals, and so on.

    Help your child create a new book using the animal scrapbook as an example. For example: *Brown Bear, Brown Bear, What Do You Feel? Brown Bear, Brown Bear, What Do You Taste? Brown Bear, Brown Bear, What Do You Hear?* Or, create a book using a member of the family. For example: *Mommy, Mommy, What Do You See?*

Related Children's Books

Colors by John J. Reiss
Harold and the Purple Crayon by Crockett Johnson
I Never Saw a Purple Cow by Emma Clark
Little Red Hen by Paul Galdone
Mystery of the Blue Paint by Steven Kellogg
Tom's Rainbow Walk by Catherine Anhott
Where Does the Brown Bear Go? by Nicki Weiss

8

Bugs

Nancy Winslow Parker and Joan Richards Wright
New York: Mulberry, 1987

Story Summary

A fascinating examination of 15 common insects, this book is a creative look into the world of these tiny creatures. Rich and colorful illustrations and a mix of fiction and nonfiction make this an engaging text.

Discussion Questions

1. Of all the bugs mentioned in the book, which one is your favorite? Why?

2. How many of the bugs described in the book have you seen around your house or neighborhood? Which one frightens you the most?

3. Why are some people afraid of bugs? Why do people try to rid their homes of bugs?

Activities (Please select one or more activities.)

1. Ask your child to select one of the insects mentioned in the book or another bug of his or her own choosing. Invite your child to demonstrate the movement of that insect in a designated area. For example, for a mosquito your child can extend his or her arms and "buzz" around the room; for a centipede your child can wriggle across the room. Provide opportunities for your child to describe the movements and why those movements may be unique to each selected insect.

2. Invite your child to begin a logbook of the number of selected bugs located in a specific area (a room in the house, a section of the classroom, a plot of land in the backyard). Encourage your child to record numbers of bugs observed during a designated part of each day (e.g., from 3:30 to 4:00) over a selected period of time (e.g., one week).

3. After your child has read the book ask him or her to create a make-believe insect that is yet to be discovered. Have your child illustrate, name, and describe the make-believe insect in writing (where the insect would live, what it would eat, if it is helpful or pesky, etc.).

Related Children's Books

Ants by Angel Julivert
The Golden Book of Insects and Spiders by Lawrence Pringle
The Grouchy Ladybug by Eric Carle
Insects Do the Strangest Things by L. Hornblow and A. Hornblow
Wasps at Home by Bianca Lavies

9

Caleb & Kate

William Steig
New York: Farrar, Straus & Giroux, 1986

Story Summary

This is a story about Caleb the carpenter and Kate the weaver. A witch puts a spell on Caleb while he is sleeping and changes him into a dog. Caleb, now a dog, shows up at Kate's front door. The spell eventually ends and the couple is reunited.

Discussion Questions

1. Would you want to be a dog?
2. How did Caleb and Kate change from the beginning of the story to the end of the story?
3. Suppose Kate asked you to help her search for her husband. How would you have answered her?
4. Pretend you were the witch. What spell would you have put on Caleb?

Activities (Please select one or more activities.)

1. Show your child the cover of the book and ask him or her to guess what the story is about. What clues are there that help with the prediction?

2. Have your child look through several old magazines for pictures of various animals. Cut out several of these pictures and paste them onto individual sheets of paper. Ask your child to put those animals that are pets into one group and those animals that live in the wild into another group. Afterwards, ask your child to put into one group those animals that have fur and into another group those animals that have feathers. Create as many groups as desired.

3. Work with your child to create make-believe animals. Obtain balloons and inflate them. Dip strips of newspaper into liquid starch and cover a balloon with two or three layers. When dry, have your child paint the features of an imaginary (or real) animal on the newspaper. Hang the finished animal in your child's room.

4. Talk with your child about what might have taken place after Caleb and Kate were finally reunited. Invite your child to draw pictures of these later events as a sequel to the story. Post the pictures in a special place.

Related Children's Books

Clifford the Big Red Dog by Norman Bridwell
The Comeback Dog by Jane R. Thomas
Harry the Dirty Dog by Gene Zion

10

The Cat in the Hat

Dr. Seuss
New York: Random House, 1957

Story Summary

Two children meet an unusual cat who tells them about some games they can play. He ends up destroying the house but returns to clean up the mess. The children wonder if they should tell their mother what happened.

Discussion Questions

1. If you were one of the children, would you tell your mother what happened?

2. What are some things you like to do on rainy days?

3. What are Things One and Two? Would you want to have them as pets?

4. Did the children's mother suspect that anything special had happened on that day? Would your mother suspect anything? Why?

Activities (Please select one or more activities.)

1. Talk with your child about some of the things that could be done or games that could be played if he or she were to stay alone in the house for an entire day. You and your child may want to put together a "Busy Box"—a collection of games and activities that can be played when your child is alone.

2. With your child, find an old pair of socks. Supply your child with materials such as yarn, buttons, sequins, paint, and glue. Using these materials, work with your child to construct simple hand puppets of Things One and Two. With your child, put on a puppet show for the family.

3. Look through several old magazines and identify several pictures of cats. Have your child cut out these pictures and paste them all on one large sheet of paper. Ask your child to title this poster and print the title along the top of the poster. Ask your child to circle the picture of the cat that most resembles the Cat in the Hat. Hang the poster in a special place.

4. Talk with your child about some of his or her daily chores. Create a simple chart that allows your child to check off each chore as it is done over the course of one or two weeks. Periodically talk with your child about the importance of every family member doing regular chores.

Related Children's Books by Dr. Seuss

And to Think That I Saw It on Mulberry Street
Did I Ever Tell You How Lucky You Are?
The 500 Hats of Bartholomew Cubbins
Horton Hatches the Egg
If I Ran the Zoo

11

A Chair for My Mother

Vera B. Williams
New York: Greenwillow, 1982

Story Summary

A young girl wants to purchase a chair for her mother, who works hard at a local diner. Although a fire destroys their home, the girl is eventually able to realize her dream.

Discussion Questions

1. Would you want to save money to buy something? What?

2. Why is it important to save money for something you really want?

3. How would you feel if you lost your belongings in a fire?

4. Why is it important to help other people?

5. Why did the neighbors want to help the family by giving them clothes and furniture?

Activities (Please select one or more activities.)

1. Ask your child to draw a picture of a favorite chair. Is it a chair in the house or a chair in a furniture store or magazine advertisement? What makes that chair so special?

2. Have your child write advertisements, in a newspaper-type format, for a favorite restaurant. It may be helpful for your child to refer to newspaper and magazine advertisements.

3. Take a field trip to a nearby furniture store and have your child "test" several chairs. Upon returning home, have your child write a brief description of the chair he or she liked the most.

4. Read the story *Goldilocks and the Three Bears* to your child. Talk about the similarities between Goldilocks trying out the chairs in the three bears' house and the family in *A Chair for My Mother* trying out all the chairs in the furniture stores.

5. With your child, review the fire exits in your house. Work with your child to prepare a safety guide for the entire family on what to do in case of a fire. Have your child draw illustrations of exits and write or dictate escape procedures.

Related Children's Books

Benjy Goes to a Restaurant by Jill Krementz
My Daddy Don't Go to Work by Madeena Spray Nolan
Something Special for Me by Vera B. Williams
Stringbean's Trip to the Shining Sea by Vera B. Williams
Three Days on a River in a Red Canoe by Vera B. Williams
Tight Times by Barbara Shook Hazen

Charlie and the Chocolate Factory

Roald Dahl

New York: Penguin, 1964

Story Summary

Chocolate, chocolate, and more chocolate! This is the story of a poor boy who wins a tour of Willy Wonka's Chocolate Factory. Adventure ensues behind the secret doors of the factory.

Discussion Questions

1. Would you want to win the "golden ticket"?
2. Did Charlie deserve to win? Why?
3. Out of the five main characters who went on the tour, which did you like most? Explain.
4. Had Willy Wonka been planning his scheme from the beginning?

Activities (Please select one or more activities.)

1. You and your child may enjoy making chocolate candy. You will need a block of pure unsweetened chocolate (or chocolate chips), a Crock Pot, a metal spoon, and molds to make miniature candy bars (available at many hobby stores or in the cooking sections of department stores). Put the chocolate into a Crock Pot set at "medium" or "low." Stir the chocolate until it is melted. Using a metal spoon, scoop the chocolate into the candy molds. Place the molds into the refrigerator. Once the chocolate has become solid again (7 to 8 minutes), turn the molds upside down and shake out the candy pieces.

2. After completing activity 1, have your child design an original wrapper for the candy. Provide your child with construction paper, markers, crayons, and other art materials and invite him or her to invent an original candy bar wrapper.

3. Take a field trip to a nearby candy factory. Discuss with your child any similarities or differences between the candy factory and the chocolate factory in the book.

4. Ask your child to create a design for the winning tickets as well as for the fraudulent ticket. Provide your child with foil paper, magic markers, and other art materials.

Related Children's Books

Chocolate Mouse and Sugar Pig by Irina Hale
Cocoa Beans and Daisies by Allamand Pascale
Grandfather Twilight by Barbara Benger
Grandpa by Barbara Borack
The Poor Boy Who Followed His Stars by Robert Graves
Rich Boy, Poor Boy by Robert Bulla

13

Charlotte's Web

E. B. White
New York: Harper & Row, 1952

Story Summary

This is a timeless story about friendships, relationships, and the responsibilities we have for one another. It is the story of Wilbur the pig and his friend Charlotte the spider.

Discussion Questions

1. What might have happened if Charlotte and Wilbur had not become friends?

2. What might have been the result if Wilbur had kept running when he escaped from his yard?

3. Wilbur knew he could never forget Charlotte. He loved her children and grandchildren, but none of them could ever take Charlotte's place. Why did Wilbur feel so strongly about Charlotte?

4. Would you want Wilbur as a pet? Why?

5. If you were the author of the book, would you change the ending? Explain.

Activities (Please select one or more activities.)

1. Encourage your child to research spiders at the library. Your child may enjoy creating a mini-book filled with interesting facts and drawings of spiders to share with the family.

2. Encourage your child to design a poster advertising Zuckerman's famous pig. Provide your child with posterboard, construction paper, glue, scissors, crayons, and markers. Hang the poster in a special place.

3. Encourage your child to research pigs at the library. Invite your child to become the family's expert on pigs. Have family members ask questions about the life, diet, and habits of a pig.

4. Encourage your child to make a timeline to show the important events of this story. A long strip of blank paper can be used to record significant events in chronological order.

5. Encourage your child to develop commercials to advertise this book to others. What kind of commercial would be appropriate for play on a local radio station?

Related Children's Books

Cricket in Times Square by George Seldon
Fantastic Mr. Fox by Roald Dahl
Mrs. Frisby and the Rats of NIMH by Robert O'Brien
Pearl's Promise by Frank Asch
Pigs Might Fly by Dick King-Smith
Warton and Morton by Russell Ericson

14

Chicken Soup with Rice

Maurice Sendak
New York: Harper & Row, 1962

Story Summary

A young boy takes the reader through each season of the year as he relates monthly activities to eating chicken soup with rice.

Discussion Questions

1. What kinds of soup do you like? Which kinds do you dislike?
2. What month or season do you enjoy most? Why?
3. What foods do you enjoy eating year round?
4. When would be the best time to eat chicken soup with rice?

Activities (Please select one or more activities.)

1. Have your child begin a collection of favorite soup recipes. Work with your child to prepare a letter to friends and relatives, asking them to send their favorite soup recipes. As recipes arrive, have your child collect them into a scrapbook. Periodically, select one of the recipes and prepare it with your child.

2. Discuss with your child where he or she might want to go on vacation. With your child, look through old magazines and cut out pictures of favorite vacation spots. Paste the pictures onto sheets of paper and ask your child to identify and label each place.

3. With your child, look through several magazines for soup advertisements. Work with your child to design an original advertisement for one of the canned soups you have at home. Encourage your child to try to "sell" the soup to other family members.

4. Work with your child to turn the refrigerator door into a "Seasons" bulletin board. Locate pictures of each of the four seasons in magazines (e.g., pictures of leaves for fall, pictures of snowflakes for winter, etc.). Help your child cut out these pictures and tape them to the refrigerator door. Ask your child to dictate a short sentence for each picture. Write the sentences on separate pieces of paper and tape them next to the pictures. Encourage your child to add additional pictures and additional sentences as desired.

Related Children's Books

Chicken Riddle by Ann Bishop
Chicken Stew by Peter Firmin
In the Night Kitchen by Maurice Sendak
Seven Little Monsters by Maurice Sendak
The Very Hungry Caterpillar by Eric Carle
The World of Chickens by Jennifer Coldrey

15

Cloudy with a Chance of Meatballs

Judi Barrett
New York: Macmillan, 1978

Story Summary

In the land of Chewandswallow, the weather occurs three times a day: breakfast, lunch, and dinner. The weather brings showers of food and drink for the people, until the day when the weather changes. It rains massive quantities of food and forces the people of Chewandswallow to find a new land to call their home.

Discussion Questions

1. How would you feel if you did not have the choice of what to eat for breakfast, lunch, and dinner?

2. What would it be like if you were forced to leave your country and begin a new life in a strange land?

3. How did the people of Chewandswallow feel when they moved to the new land and had to go shopping for their food?

4. If you had to leave the country, what would you take with you? Why?

Activities (Please select one or more activities.)

1. Talk with your child about some major food groups (e.g., milk and eggs, fruit and vegetables, grain and bread, meat and fish). Ask your child to list the titles of the food groups at the top of a large sheet of paper. Have your child list the foods in the book according to food groups. Which food group has the most items? Do the people of Chewandswallow eat balanced meals? What must be done to ensure them a balanced diet?

2. Take your child to a supermarket. Ask your child to locate the prices of all the foods mentioned in the story. Invite your child to calculate the cost of a sample meal as illustrated in the book. Have your child calculate what it would cost to make a dinner of his or her choice.

3. In the story, there is a newspaper with current events. Have your child create a "Food Newspaper" about food, cooking, meals, and other eating events that take place at home. How can dinner become a sporting event? How can breakfast become front-page news? How can lunch become a business section?

Related Children's Books

Climate and Weather by Laurie Bolwell
Dragon Smoke by Lilian Moore
Hurricanes and Twisters by Irving Adler
The Missing Tarts by B. G. Hennessey
On Sunday the Wind Came by Alan C. Elliot
The Rain Cloud by Mary Rayner
The Riddle King's Food Riddles by Mike Thaler
So Hungry! by Harriet Ziefert
World of Weather by David A. Adler

Corduroy

Don Freeman
New York: Viking, 1968

Story Summary

Corduroy is a teddy bear who is missing a button on his green corduroy bib-overalls. One day a little girl notices him in the store window and wants to buy him. After she takes him home, he feels like he is in a palace.

Discussion Questions

1. Why is Corduroy such a special bear?

2. Why did the little girl pick Corduroy over all the other beautiful toys?

3. How did Corduroy feel when he left the store?

4. Is there a toy that you own that is very special to you? Why is it special?

5. What might have happened to Corduroy if the little girl had not found him?

Activities (Please select one or more activities.)

1. Take your child on a "field trip" to a toy store. Talk about what makes some toys more valuable than others (other than price). Help your child understand that cost is not necessarily equivalent to value. On your return home, have your child write what he or she thought was the most important part of the trip.

2. Have your child create "Have You Seen This Bear?" posters. Hang these posters around the house.

3. You and your child may enjoy making bear cookies. Locate a bear-shaped cookie cutter and use the following recipe:

Bear Cookies

2 cups butter	5 cups flour
3 cups confectioners' sugar	2 teaspoons baking soda
2 eggs	2 teaspoons cream of tartar
2 teaspoons vanilla	½ teaspoon salt

Cream butter and sugar. Add eggs and vanilla. Mix the dry ingredients together and add to the creamed mixture. Patiently mix with hands or electric mixer (the mixture will be very dry). Roll the dough to desired thickness. Cut out bear cookies and decorate with colored sugar, raisins, nuts, and so on. Bake at 350 degrees for 12 to 15 minutes.

Eat and enjoy!!

Related Children's Books

Bear Goes Shopping by Harriet Ziefert
The Forgotten Bear by Consuelo Joerns
Friends by Helen Oxenbury

The Night It Rained Toys by Dorothy Stephenson
The Secret World of Teddy Bears by Pamela Prince
Teach Me About Friends by Joy Berry

17

The Day Jimmy's Boa Ate the Wash

Trinka Hakes Noble
New York: Dial, 1980

Story Summary

A boring class trip to the farm turns into an uproariously funny series of events involving cows, pigs, an egg fight, a busload of children, and, of course, a boa constrictor.

Discussion Questions

1. Why was the girl apathetic about the class trip?

2. What will the farmer and his wife do with the boa constrictor?

3. What was the funniest part of the story? Why?

4. What will Jimmy do with his new pet pig?

5. Would your friends enjoy this book? Why?

Activities (Please select one or more activities.)

1. Obtain discarded panty hose or nylon stockings. Work with your child to stuff one stocking with cloth scraps or crumpled newspaper. Paint a face on one end to create a boa constrictor. Have your child manipulate the boa constrictor while you retell the story.

2. Call the biology department of a local college or university and ask if they have any snakes on display. Find out if it would be possible for you and your child to view any snakes and talk with a professor about snakes and how they live.

3. Work with your child to write a story titled "The Day the Boa Came to Our School."

4. Draw the outlines of several different items of clothing (shirts, pants, shoes, etc.) on pieces of construction paper and cut them out. Tie a piece of string between two places in your child's room. Ask your child to write one important word from the story on each piece of "clothing." Use clothespins to clip the words to the string. Occasionally ask your child to use one of the words in an original sentence.

5. You and your child might enjoy reading other books by this author, including *Apple Tree Christmas*, *Hansy's Mermaid*, *The King's Tea*, and *Meanwhile Back at the Ranch*.

Related Children's Books

Crictor by Tomi Ungerer
Python's Party by Brian Wildsmith
Slithers by Syd Hoff
The Snake by Bernard Waber
Snakes by Leonard Appleby
Snakes Are Hunters by Patricia Lauber
To Bathe a Boa by Imbior Kudrna

18

Dear Mr. Henshaw

Beverly Cleary
New York: Morrow, 1983

Story Summary

Leigh Botts writes to his favorite book author, Mr. Henshaw. His letters are filled with questions and advice as well as revealing information about Leigh's life, his thoughts, and his feelings about his mother and father. *Dear Mr. Henshaw* won the Newbery Award in 1984.

Discussion Questions

1. What author would you want to write to? Why?

2. Would you want to have a pen pal? Why?

3. How is Leigh's life similar to or different from your life?

4. What questions would you want to ask Beverly Cleary, the author of this book?

5. Why would Leigh want to tell things about his family to a person he had never met?

Activities (Please select one or more activities.)

1. Have your child create a booklet entitled "How to Become a Better Writer." Ask your child to interview adults, teachers, business people, reporters, and other children in the community on the tips and strategies that help people write. Assemble the collected information into booklet form to share with the family.

2. Have your child write to relatives, grandparents, and friends who live in different cities, states, and countries and ask for postcards from their area. Encourage your child to share the postcards with the family. As postcards arrive, your child may want to assemble them into an attractive display or bulletin board.

3. Your child may want to prepare a letter to Beverly Cleary commenting on this book or other books she has written. Your child may want to include questions about the writing of children's books or about writing in general. Send the letter in care of Ms. Cleary's publisher (William Morrow and Co., 105 Madison Avenue, New York, NY 10016). Advise your child that he or she may not receive a personal reply because Ms. Cleary receives so many letters that she cannot reply to all of them herself. (Beverly Cleary's birthday is April 12. Your child may want to send her a birthday card.)

4. Your child might enjoy watching the development and growth of butterflies. Nasco (901 Janesville Avenue, Fort Atkinson, WI 53538; 1-800-558-9595) produces a "Butterfly Garden," which can be ordered through their catalog or found in many toy and hobby stores. Your child will be able to observe and record the growth of butterflies from cocoons to adults.

Related Children's Books by Beverly Cleary

Ellen Tibbits

Henry & Ribsy

Henry Huggins

The Mouse & the Motorcycle

Ramona Quimby, Age 8

Ramona the Pest

Runaway Ralph

19

Doctor DeSoto

William Steig
New York: Scholastic, 1982

Story Summary

This is a tale of wit versus might. Dr. and Mrs. DeSoto run the best dental clinic in town. Though the DeSotos are tiny mice, they work on patients as big as cows. One day Dr. DeSoto decides to help a big fox who is in pain. The fox experiences more than he had expected.

Discussion Questions

1. What strategy would you have used to "outfox" the fox if you were Dr. DeSoto?

2. How might the story have ended if Mrs. DeSoto's plan had not worked?

3. What other animals would be a threat to Dr. and Mrs. DeSoto?

4. Would you want Dr. DeSoto to be your dentist? Why?

Activities (Please select one or more activities.)

1. As you read the story, stop at the part where Mrs. DeSoto says, "I have a plan." Invite your child to predict what will happen next and to write down his or her prediction. Finish the story and talk with your child about the prediction and the actual ending.

2. Visit your family dentist and ask him or her to talk to your child about proper dental care. Collect any available brochures and discuss them with your child. Invite your child to develop an original brochure on dental care for children.

3. Discuss with your child how our diet would be different if we did not have teeth. Have your child make a list of foods that must be chewed and a list of foods that can be swallowed without chewing. Which list is longer?

4. Obtain "kitchen oven-fired" clay or "air dry" clay from a hobby, variety, or art store. Work with your child to create an oversized model of a tooth. Display the tooth for the family to see.

5. You and your child may enjoy reading other books by William Steig, including *The Amazing Bone*, *Sylvester and the Magic Pebble*, and *The Real Thief*.

Related Children's Books

Arthur's Tooth by Marc Brown
The Bear's Toothache by David McPhail
Fox Eyes by Margaret Wise Brown
Rosie's Walk by Pat Hutchins

20

East of the Sun and West of the Moon

Mercer Mayer
New York: Macmillan, 1980

Story Summary

The beautiful daughter of a farmer and his wife faces hardship when her father becomes ill and she must seek water from the South Wind. A frog assists her in return for three wishes. When the frog wishes to marry her, she refuses and kills the frog. A spell is broken and the frog turns into a handsome youth, who is taken away to the Land of East of the Sun and West of the Moon to wed the Troll Princess. The maiden travels in search of her love with the help of enchanting creatures along the way.

Discussion Questions

1. What might have happened if the maiden had turned into a frog? What would the youth have done?

2. The frog was to ask for three wishes, but only asked two. What might have been the third wish?

3. How would the story have been different if the youth had been a different animal, such as a cat, rabbit, or giraffe, instead of a frog?

4. Is it always important to keep a promise? Why?

Activities (Please select one or more activities.)

1. Invite your child to check the library for other versions of this story, including "East of the Sun and West of the Moon" in *Norwegian Folk Tales* by P. C. Asbjørnsen and Jørgon E. Moe (New York: Viking, 1960), *East of the Sun and West of the Moon* by Kathleen Hague and Michael Hague (San Diego: Harcourt Brace Jovanovich, 1980), or *East of the Sun and West of the Moon: A Play* by Nancy Willard (San Diego: Harcourt Brace Jovanovich, 1989). Discuss similarities and differences.

2. Your child may want to grow his or her own frogs. Kits are available from Holcombs Educational Materials (3205 Harvard Avenue, Cleveland, OH 44105; 1-800-321-2543). Kit #998-0125H is priced at $14.95 (at this writing) and includes a container, food, instructions, and a coupon for live tadpoles. Check your local teacher supply store for similar kits.

3. Encourage your child to build his or her version of a troll palace. Invite your child to obtain recycled materials such as milk cartons, cereal boxes, tin cans, and bottles. Supply glue, paint, string, and other art materials to complete the project.

4. Your child might enjoy creating trolls from homemade clay: Mix 1 cup flour and ½ cup salt. Add ⅓ cup water, a little at a time. Mix the dough by hand until it is smooth. Form into shapes. Let air dry or bake at 225 degrees for 30 minutes. Paint with tempera paint.

Related Children's Books

East of the Sun and West of the Moon by Kathleen Hague and Michael Hague
East of the Sun and West of the Moon: A Play by Nancy Willard
Favorite Fairy Tales Told in Norway by Virginia Haviland
Norwegian Folk Tales by P. C. Asbjørnsen and Jørgen E. Moe

21

Fly Away Home

Eve Bunting
New York: Clarion, 1991

Story Summary

This is a poignant story about a young boy and his father who are homeless and live in an airport. Filled with hope and determination for a better life, the boy and his father elude security people, obtain food, and learn to survive by their wits. This is a wonderful "read-aloud" story for parents and children to share and discuss together.

Discussion Questions

1. Why did the author include the little story about the bird trapped inside the airport?

2. What series of events do you think led to the boy and his father living in the airport?

3. What will the boy and his father need to do to move into their own apartment?

4. Do you think the events of this story happen on a regular basis? Explain.

Activities (Please select one or more activities.)

1. Talk with your child about homeless people in this country. What events cause people or families to become homeless? Should we treat homeless people any differently than we do people who live in houses or apartments? What are the events that could cause a family to become homeless? How can we help homeless people?

2. Visit a homeless shelter or social service agency and ask about the services provided for homeless individuals and families. You and your child may want to volunteer to assist homeless people.

3. Invite your child to write a letter to the editor about the plight of homeless people in this country. Encourage your child to address the fact that homelessness does not just happen to those of low socioeconomic standing—it affects people from many walks of life.

4. Encourage your child to write a fictitious letter to the young boy in the story. What words of support could your child share with the boy that would give him hope for a better future?

Related Children's Books by Eve Bunting

The Empty Window
Ghost's Hour, Spook's Hour
How Many Days to America? A Thanksgiving Story
The Wall
The Wednesday Surprise

22

Frog and Toad Are Friends

Arnold Lobel
New York: Harper & Row, 1970

Story Summary

This collection of five short stories revolves around the coming of spring, a special story, a missing button, a funny bathing suit, and an important letter.

Discussion Questions

1. Why are Frog and Toad such good friends?

2. What does the word *friendship* mean to you?

3. What are some of the special things friends do for each other?

4. Which of the five stories did you enjoy most? Why?

5. If you could say anything to Frog and Toad, what would you say?

Activities (Please select one or more activities.)

1. You and your child may want to create a "Frog and Toad Museum." Collect several of the items mentioned in the stories (e.g., buttons, a letter, a bathing suit, etc.). Place them in a large, flat box (e.g., a bakery box) and remove the lid. Label each item according to the story title. Cover the open box with plastic wrap to create a display resembling a museum case.

2. Work with your child to create a new adventure for Frog and Toad. Your child may want to dictate or write an original story to share with the family.

3. Encourage your child to write a letter to Toad. What would your child want to say? Make a mailbox from a milk carton or small box and paint it red and blue. Write a letter from Toad to respond to your child.

4. Ask your child to make a list of different animals (e.g., tigers, bears, cats, etc.) used to advertise products such as cereals, cars, and toys. Do any commercial products use frogs or toads as symbols?

5. Your child might enjoy reading other books about Frog and Toad by Arnold Lobel, including *Frog and Toad All Year*, *Days with Frog and Toad*, and *The Frog and Toad Pop-Up Book*.

Related Children's Books

Alexander and the Wind-Up Mouse by Leo Lionni
Best Friends by Steven Kellogg
Commander Toad in Space by Jane Yolen
Frog on His Own by Mercer Mayer
George and Martha by James Marshall
Petunia by Roger Duvoisin

Galimoto

Karen Lynn Williams
New York: Lothrop, 1990

Story Summary

Kondi, a seven-year-old boy who lives in southeastern Africa in the country of Malawi, wants to make a galimoto (a homemade car built by children). After resourcefully gathering enough materials, he is able to construct a pickup truck. Upon completion, his friends cheer him on as he glides it over a dusty path.

Discussion Questions

1. What elements of your personality are similar to Kondi's personality? How are you different?
2. What materials do you have immediately available that could be used to construct a homemade car?
3. How is Kondi's everyday life similar to your life?
4. Would you want to have Kondi as a friend? Explain.

Activities (Please select one or more activities.)

1. Talk with your child about the saying "Necessity is the mother of invention." Discuss the importance of imagination in the process of invention.
2. Invite your child to compare Kondi's village to your town in a chart on a large sheet of blank newsprint or posterboard. Divide the paper vertically. Label one column "Kondi's Village" and the other column "My Town." Have your child record specific features, characteristics, and landmarks. Discuss differences and similarities.
3. Provide your child with a map or globe of the world. Locate Malawi and have your child calculate the distance from your state to Malawi. How long would it take to fly there at 550 miles per hour? What forms of transportation (in addition to airplanes) would be needed to travel from your town to Kondi's village?

Related Children's Books

At the Crossroads by Rachel Isadora
Charlie's House by Reviva Schermbruker
Jambo Means Hello by Muriel Feelings
The Rains Are Coming by Sanna Stanley
When Africa Was Home by Karen Lynn Williams
Why Mosquitoes Buzz in People's Ears by Verna Aardema
Why the Sun and the Moon Live in the Sky by Elphenstone Dayrell

Gila Monsters Meet You at the Airport

Marjorie Sharmat
New York: Aladdin, 1980

Story Summary

This is a riotous tale about a young boy who is moving from New York City "out west," where there are lots of cactus and plenty of buffalo, and everybody says "Howdy." This book is a humorous portrayal of the misconceptions youngsters have about other parts of the country and the people who live there.

Discussion Questions

1. What did you enjoy most about this book? What made you laugh the loudest?

2. What are some facts or features about where you live that people in other parts of the country might not understand?

3. How could the main character have come to believe what he did about life "out west"?

4. What would be the biggest change if you lived in another part of the country?

Activities (Please select one or more activities.)

1. Provide your child with a map of the United States. Invite your child to locate some of the places mentioned in the book (not all are identified) and mark them on the map (this can be done with small strips of masking tape). Encourage your child to measure the distance between New York City and "out west."

2. Visit a video store and obtain a video of a different part of the country (travel videos and videos by the National Geographic Society are frequently available for rent). Watch the video with your child and discuss some of the similarities and differences between that part of the country and where you live. Your child may want to construct a chart of these similarities and differences.

3. Invite your child to select a place in the United States where he or she would want to live. Encourage your child to collect information from the library about that location or write to the department of tourism in that state to obtain brochures and other information. Invite your child to share with the family a report titled "A New Place to Live."

Related Children's Books

Clyde Monster by Robert Crowe
Ira Says Goodbye by Bernard Waber
Ira Sleeps Over by Bernard Waber
Mitchell Is Moving by Marjorie Sharmat
There's a Monster Under My Bed by James Howe
Today Was a Terrible Day by Patricia Reilly Giff

25

The Gingerbread Boy

Paul Galdone
Boston: Houghton Mifflin, 1975

Story Summary

An old lady bakes a delightful gingerbread boy, but he runs away. No one can catch him, except for a very crafty fox who gets the last laugh . . . or rather, the last bite!

Discussion Questions

1. Are there certain people you should trust and other people you should not trust?
2. What might have happened if the fox had not been able to outsmart the gingerbread boy?
3. Why did the author write this story?
4. If you were asked to write a new ending for the story, what would you change? Why?
5. Would you enjoy reading this book again?

Activities (Please select one or more activities.)

1. Purchase a box of gingerbread mix from your grocery store. Work with your child to make gingerbread cookies or gingerbread boys. Your child may enjoy reenacting the story using a gingerbread boy cookie as a prop.
2. Have your child create a gingerbread boy from construction paper, buttons, glue, and glitter.
3. Have your child dictate or write a sequel to the story with the premise that the gingerbread boy was able to escape from the fox.
4. You and your child may enjoy recording an audio version of this story. Alternate parts and record various sections of the book.
5. Invite your child to create a song about the gingerbread boy. Have your child choose a popular tune such as "Row, Row, Row Your Boat" or "She'll Be Comin' 'Round the Mountain," write new lyrics for the music, and sing the song for the family.
6. Write the word *gingerbread* on a large sheet of paper. Work with your child to form smaller words using the letters in *gingerbread* (e.g., bad, need, read, grab, ring).

Related Children's Books by Paul Galdone

The Little Red Hen
The Monkey and the Crocodile
Three Aesop Fox Fables
The Three Billy Goats Gruff
The Three Little Pigs

The Giving Tree

Shel Silverstein
New York: HarperCollins, 1964

Story Summary

This is a tale about the relationship between a young boy and an apple tree. The boy and the tree enjoy each other's company, but as the boy grows up he takes apples, branches, and the trunk to satisfy his needs. At the end of the story, the tree has been reduced to a stump and the boy has become a very old man—each with nothing more to give. This is a wonderful allegory about the responsibilities a human being has for living organisms in the environment.

Discussion Questions

1. Do you have a special plant, tree, or pet? How do you care for that plant or animal?

2. Why should human beings take care of the plants and animals?

3. What do plants provide for us?

4. If all the plants were destroyed, could human beings survive? Explain.

Activities (Please select one or more activities.)

1. You and your child may enjoy planting and tending a special tree. Visit a gardening center or nursery and talk with the personnel about an appropriate native variety of tree. Select a tree and plant it in a designated place in your yard (or perhaps a neighborhood park). Encourage your child to care for the tree according to instructions provided by the nursery personnel.

2. With your child, visit a grocery store and make a list of all the products available from trees (e.g., fruits, nuts, paper, etc.). Encourage your child to make a list of the products used in your home that can be obtained from trees. Discuss the implications for humanity if we could not obtain these products from trees.

3. Have your child visit a public library or school library and obtain information on the care of trees. Invite your child to write a brief brochure or newsletter specifically for children on the care of trees. What information should be included to ensure the health of several varieties of local trees?

Related Children's Books

The Ever-Living Tree by Linda Vieira
Green Giants by Sneed Collard
Sky Tree by Thomas Locker
The Tree in the Ancient Forest by Carol Reed-Jones

27

The Glorious Flight

Alice Provensen and Martin Provensen
New York: Viking, 1983

Story Summary

This is a wonderful biography of Louis Bleriot, whose fascination with flying machines produced the *Bleriot XI*, an airplane that crossed the English Channel in 37 minutes in the early 1900s.

Discussion Questions

1. What are some similarities and differences between life in the early 1900s and life today?
2. Why do people enjoy flying?
3. What would be the most adventurous part about taking an airplane trip today?
4. If Louis Bleriot flew across the English Channel today, how would the trip be different?
5. If you could visit any place in the world, where would you go? Why? What kind of transportation would you use?

Activities (Please select one or more activities.)

1. Visit a public library with your child. Ask the librarian for books on the history of aviation or airplanes. After doing research at the library, you and your child may want to build a model of an early airplane (available at hobby stores).
2. Have your child pretend to be a news reporter who has been assigned to interview Louis Bleriot. Have your child write down questions to ask Bleriot.
3. Invite your child to create posters and advertisements encouraging people to fly across the English Channel. What information should be included? Should illustrations be used? Will there be a reward?
4. Have your child imagine that he or she is Louis Bleriot, who has just arrived in England. Have your child write about England in a journal or travel log, noting first impressions, landmarks, weather, and so on. Your child might want to reflect on the journey: What did it feel like to fly? What was seen?
5. Help your child construct different types of paper airplanes and decorate them. Test the airplanes outside. Discuss why particular paper airplanes fly farther than others, and encourage your child to think about the development and progression of Bleriot's planes (*Bleriot I* through *Bleriot XI*).

Related Children's Books

Cars, Boats, and Planes by Ed Emberley
Famous Planes by Brenda Thompson
The First Book of Airplanes by Jeanne Bendick
Record-Breaking Airplanes by Don Berliner
Up, Up, and Away by Margaret Hillert
Wizard McBean and His Flying Machine by Dennis Nolan

Goodnight Moon

Margaret Wise Brown
New York: Harper & Row, 1947

Story Summary

This is the story of a baby rabbit's bedtime ritual. He goes to sleep in the "Great Green Room" and bids goodnight to all his favorite things.

Discussion Questions

1. What do you enjoy doing just before bedtime?

2. How would your life be different if you slept during the day and awoke at night?

3. Why did the rabbit say goodnight to so many things?

4. What would you change in this story if you were the author? If you were the main character, would you have done anything differently?

Activities (Please select one or more activities.)

1. Discuss bedtime rituals with your child. Make a list of the things your child likes to do just before bed (e.g., line up shoes, hang up clothes, put away toys, brush teeth, read a favorite book). Print the activities on index cards (one activity per card). Shuffle the cards and have your child put them into the correct order.

2. Talk with your child about noises that can be heard at night in and around the house. You and your child may want to record these sounds. Talk with your child about scary sounds at night: What makes a sound scary?

3. Talk with your child about occupations that require people to work at night. Make a list of these jobs, including illustrations, pictures, and brief job descriptions. Discuss the differences between nighttime and daytime jobs.

4. Visit a public library and obtain recordings of several lullabies. Encourage your child to sing along as you play the recordings. Talk with your child about the differences among the songs. You may want to use *The Lullaby Songbook* by Jane Yolen (New York: Harcourt Brace, 1986) as a reference.

Related Children's Books

Bedtime for Frances by Russell Hoban
Good Night Richard Rabbit by Robert Kraus
Goodnight Max by Hanne Turk
Lullabies and Night Songs by William Engvick
Moonlight by Jan Ormerod
What the Moon Is Like by Franklyn M. Branley

29

The Great Kapok Tree

Lynne Cherry
New York: Gulliver, 1990

Story Summary

This is the story of a young man who enters the rain forest to cut down a Kapok tree. He becomes tired and weak from the heat, sits down to rest, and falls asleep. While he sleeps, the animals of the forest whisper in his ear not to cut down the Kapok tree. Each animal has a different reason for saving the tree.

Discussion Questions

1. If you could be one of the animals in the story, which one would you be? Why?
2. What would happen if all the rain forests were destroyed?
3. What can children do to protect the rain forests?
4. How do trees affect your life?

Activities (Please select one or more activities.)

1. Invite your child to write to environmental groups and request information, newsletters, brochures, and facts about the world's rain forests and efforts to protect these valuable areas.

   Children's Rainforest
   P.O. Box 936
   Lewiston, ME 04240

   Save the Rainforest
   604 Jamie Street
   Dodgeville, WI 53533

   Rainforest Action Network
   450 Sansome Street
   Suite 700
   San Francisco, CA 94111

2. Ask your child to imagine that he or she is one of the animals in the story. Have your child create a poster titled "Save Our Home" that includes a full-color drawing of the animal and a convincing advertisement for saving the Kapok tree.

3. Invite your child to rewrite the end of the story, telling what might have happened if the man had cut down the tree. This alternative ending can be in the form of letters written from the animals, who are now homeless.

4. Invite your child to create a collage of all the animals mentioned in the story. Cut out pictures and photographs from old magazines and glue them to a sheet of posterboard or construction paper. Have your child share the collage with the family.

Related Children's Books

Exploring the Rainforest by Anthony D. Fredericks
One Day in the Tropical Rain Forest by Jean Craighead George
Rain Forest by Helen Cowcher

Tropical Rain Forests Around the World by Elaine Landau
Where the Forest Meets the Sea by Jeannie Baker
Why Save the Rain Forest? by Donald Silver

30

The Grouchy Ladybug

Eric Carle

New York: Thomas Y. Crowell, 1977

Story Summary

This is a story about a selfish and grouchy ladybug who wants to prove he is better than everyone else. In the end he discovers that sharing and friendship are more important than power.

Discussion Questions

1. What made this ladybug so grouchy?

2. If the ladybug had not been slapped by the whale's tail, what might have been the next animal the ladybug would have met?

3. What did you enjoy most about this story? Why?

4. If you were to write a letter to Eric Carle, what would you write?

Activities (Please select one or more activities.)

1. Work with your child to make a clock. Use a paper plate for the face of the clock and black construction paper for the hour and minute hands. Write numbers on the face of the clock with magic markers. Attach the hands to the face of the clock with a paper fastener. Reread the story with your child and move the clock hands to the positions indicated in the story.

2. Draw a large leaf on a piece of green construction paper. Cut out the leaf and hang it on a wall in your child's room. Have your child draw and cut out a ladybug and the other animals in the story. Retell the story. Have your child tape the appropriate cutout on the leaf as the animal is introduced in the story.

3. You and your child may want to begin an insect collection. Obtain a clean glass jar (a mayonnaise or pickle jar works best). Take a walk with your child and collect soil and a few twigs to put into the jar. Ask your child to collect several insects and put them into the jar. Upon returning home, have your child draw pictures of the insects. Discuss the similarities and differences among the insects. Release the insects (where you found them) within a few days. You and your child may want to visit a public library to obtain books about these insects (the Eyewitness Junior series from Knopf is an excellent reference).

Related Children's Books

Do You Know What Time It Is? by Roz Abisch
Ladybug, Ladybug! by Robert Kraus
Lucy Ladybug by Gladys Conklin
Tick-Tock, Let's Read the Clock by Bobbi Katz
Time by Jan Pienkowski

31

Hawk, I'm Your Brother

Byrd Baylor
New York: Macmillan, 1986

Story Summary

A Native American boy captures a hawk in the hope that he can also capture the hawk's ability to fly.

Discussion Questions

1. Why have humans been so intrigued by the flight of birds?
2. What nickname would you give to a boy who loves to fly?
3. Have you ever wished for something that was impossible to get?
4. How is the Native American understanding of nature unique?
5. Did the boy really try to find out why he could not fly?
6. Would the boy have had different interests if he had lived in the city?

Activities (Please select one or more activities.)

1. Visit a hobby store and obtain bird features. Have your child draw an outline of a bird on a piece of cardboard. Help your child glue the feathers to the outline to create a replica of a hawk.

2. Help your child make bird feeders to place around your house. A simple feeder can be made with a pine cone, peanut butter, and birdseed: Spread peanut butter over a pine cone and roll the pine cone in bird seed. Another feeder can be made from an empty milk carton: Cut a small window in the side of the carton and fill it with bird seed. Hang the feeders in a tree near a window. Have your child keep a record of the varieties of birds that visit the feeders. You and your child may want to visit a library to obtain books about bird sighting.

3. Obtain a skeletal model of a bird from a hobby or museum store. Discuss with your child the characteristics of a bird's skeleton that help it to fly (i.e., lightweight, hollow bones, etc.). Assemble the model with your child and display it in a prominent place.

4. Arrange a visit to a nearby college or university to talk to a professor in the biology or zoology department about hawks in particular or birds in general. Be sure to observe any ornithological displays.

Related Children's Books

First Came the Indians by M. J. Wheeler
I Wish I Could Fly by Ron Maris
Indian Two Feet and His Eagle Feather by Margaret Friskey
The Wishing Well by Eugene Bradley Coco

A House Is a House for Me

Mary Ann Hoberman
New York: Viking, 1978

Story Summary

This is the story of a little boy who discovers the different types of houses in the world. He explores animal houses, food houses, and human houses.

Discussion Questions

1. What type of house would you want to live in, and why? What would your house look like?

2. What are some other names for a house? How many different kinds of houses are there?

3. How are animal houses different from human houses?

Activities (Please select one or more activities.)

1. Read to your child the story *Hansel and Gretel.* Discuss real and make-believe houses. Ask your child to "invent" a house made from some type of food, such as spaghetti or swiss cheese. What would it look like? How would it be constructed? Who would live in it?

2. Ask your child to select an object in his or her room (e.g., teddy bear, toy truck, doll). Have your child construct a house for this object using crayons, markers, cardboard, pipe cleaners, glue, small boxes, tissue paper, and paint. Your child may want to display the house and its inhabitants in the family bookcase.

3. Help your child take photographs of different houses and other dwellings in your community or neighborhood. Once the pictures have been developed, help your child assemble them into a "House" scrapbook. Ask your child to title each house and paste the names alongside the pictures. Invite your child to take additional photographs of houses for the scrapbook on family vacations.

Related Children's Books

Anybody Home? by Aileen Lucia Fisher
Basis Brush Builds a House by Peter Firman
Grandma's House by Elaine Moore
The Little House by Virginia Burton
Ming Lo Moves the Mountain by Arnold Lobel
New House by Joyce Maynard

33

How My Parents Learned to Eat
Ina R. Friedman
Boston: Houghton Mifflin, 1984

Story Summary

This is the story of an American sailor stationed in Japan who begins dating a Japanese schoolgirl. When they decide to have dinner together, each learns the other's way of eating as a surprise. They fall in love and marry, incorporating both ethnic backgrounds into their kitchen.

Discussion Questions

1. If you were to visit Japan, what would you enjoy most?

2. What is the most unusual food you have ever eaten?

3. Why do people visit foreign countries?

4. Why are there are so many different ways of eating food?

Activities (Please select one or more activities.)

1. Obtain a map of Japan and help your child locate Yokohama, Japan. Have your child calculate the distance between Yokohama and your town; between Yokohama and Washington, D.C.; and between Yokohama and Tokyo.

2. Visit a public library and obtain books about Japan and Japanese culture (e.g., *Take a Trip to Japan* by Gwynneth Ashby). Discuss with your child the similarities and differences between Japanese culture and American culture.

3. Work with your child to write a humorous story explaining the functions of American eating utensils. For example: "Mr. Fork has three or four prongs that are used to pick up several types of food, such as . . . "

4. Visit an oriental restaurant and obtain a set of chopsticks for your child. Show your child the proper way to hold and use them. Have your child practice picking up small objects with the chopsticks. You may want to make this a daily activity for two weeks and have your child record in a notebook his or her improvement.

Related Children's Books

Brinkley's Japanese-English Dictionary by F. Brinkley
Dance, Dance, Amy-Chan! by Lucy Hawkinson
Eating Out by Helen Oxenbury
Meet Miki Takino by Helen Copeland
Mieko by Leo Politi
Take a Trip to Japan by Gwynneth Ashby

I Know an Old Lady

Rose Bonne
New York: Rand McNally, 1961

Story Summary

This is the delightful story of an unusual lady who has the nasty habit of swallowing animals. In the end, a horse finally does the old lady in.

Discussion Questions

1. Why did the old lady eat all the animals?
2. What would happen if you swallowed a fly?
3. What are some other animals the old lady might have swallowed?
4. What animal could the old lady have swallowed to catch the horse?

Activities (Please select one or more activities.)

1. Ask your child to select his or her favorite animal from the story. Have your child draw a picture of the old lady eating that animal. Have your child draw another picture of the animal eating the old lady. Post the two pictures side by side. Discuss any similarities and differences between the two illustrations. Ask your child how the story would be different if the animal had eaten the old lady.

2. Provide your child with modeling clay (available in hobby stores). Work with your child to make small models of each of the animals in the story. Display them in a special place.

3. Have your child look through several old magazines, cut out pictures of the animals in the story, and put together a scrapbook titled "Old Lady Animals." Your child may want to add pictures of animals not in the story that the old lady might have eaten.

4. Ask your child to tell you this story from the viewpoint of one of the animals. For example: "My name is Sammy Spider and I did not appreciate being swallowed by the Old Lady. The reason why I wriggled and wriggled and tickled inside her was because I was trying to escape." You may want to record an audio version of your child's story.

Related Children's Books

Anansi the Spider by Eric Carle
Animal Fact/Animal Fable by Seymour Simon
Animalia by Grahame Base
King of the Birds by Shirley Climo
This Is the House That Jack Built by Jack Kent
The Three Billy Goats Gruff by Paul Galdone
The Very Busy Spider by Eric Carle

35

I'm in Charge of Celebrations

Byrd Baylor
New York: Scribner's, 1986

Story Summary

In this beautifully illustrated, lyrical story, the author shares her celebrations in the southwestern desert. She celebrates 108 special days in her life, including the night she saw falling stars and the time she looked into the eyes of a coyote.

Discussion Questions

1. What are the events in your life that you would want to celebrate?

2. Why do people celebrate events such as birthdays, weddings, and anniversaries?

3. What is your favorite holiday? Why?

4. If you could create a new holiday, what would it be? What would people do on that day?

Activities (Please select one or more activities.)

1. Read the book aloud. Invite your child to listen and imagine the story with his or her eyes closed. Afterwards, invite your child to compare his or her mental images to the illustrations in the book.

2. Provide your child with a wall calendar or large desk calendar. Encourage your child to note (over an extended period of time) special events in his or her life, from getting a new tooth to vacationing in another state. Periodically discuss these events.

3. Invite your child to observe an animal (in the wild, if possible). Encourage your child to write down the events in that animal's life. What events could be classified as "celebrations" (e.g., the family dog gets a dog biscuit, a squirrel discovers a nut, etc.)?

4. Discuss the illustrations in the book. How do they convey the emotions of the author? Invite your child to illustrate one day in his or her life. Encourage your child to use colors or images that evoke special feelings (e.g., blue colors and jagged lines for a sad day).

Related Children's Books

Between Cattails by Terry Williams
The Desert Is Theirs by Byrd Baylor
Desert Voices by Byrd Baylor
Happy Birthday to You! by Dr. Seuss
How Many Days to America? A Thanksgiving Story by Eve Bunting
Mother Earth, Father Sky by Jane Yolen
Uncle Vova's Tree by Patricia Polacco

In the Year of the Boar and Jackie Robinson

Bette Bao Lord
New York: Harper & Row, 1984

Story Summary

This is the story of Shirley Temple Wong, who moves to the United States from China, slowly adjusts to the new culture, and takes an interest in the Brooklyn Dodgers. Jackie Robinson becomes her hero as she follows the Dodgers' advance to the World Series.

Discussion Questions

1. What qualities do Shirley Temple Wong and Jackie Robinson have in common?
2. Is it important that Shirley maintain her Chinese heritage?
3. How would it feel to be a student in a foreign country?
4. Why did Shirley enjoy baseball so much?

Activities (Please select one or more activities.)

1. Ask your child to create an original map of your neighborhood or community. What special features should be included? What buildings or important landmarks should be included for visitors. You and your child may be able to obtain a street map of your town or community from a bookstore or the city hall. Has your child chosen to include features that the official map excludes?

2. Discuss with your child how he or she would feel if the family had to move to a foreign country. How would your child cope with a new language, a new culture, and a different type of school? Have your child prepare an experimental "guidebook" for foreign visitors to your community. What should be included in the guide to help foreigners adjust to the neighborhood, language, customs, and schools?

3. Have your child research his or her ethnic background and the family's country of origin. Your child may want to interview older relatives about their recollections of "the old country." Does the family have documents or letters that could be used as a resource? Does the family maintain any customs or traditions from "the old country"?

4. Ask your child to prepare a travel brochure on China specifically for students in the fifth and sixth grades. Visit several travel agencies and obtain information or literature on travel to China. What would 10- and 11-year-old travelers want to know about travel and life in China?

Related Children's Books

Homesick by Jean Fritz
Introducing Shirley Braverman by Hilma Wolitzer
The Long Journey to a New Land by Joan Sandir
Maria Luisa by Winifred Madison
Thank You, Jackie Robinson by Barbara Cohen
The Voyage of the Lucky Dragon by Jack Bennett

37

Ira Sleeps Over

Bernard Waber

Boston: Houghton Mifflin, 1972

Story Summary

When Ira is invited to sleep over at his friend's house, he wonders whether to bring his teddy bear. Ira discovers that he is not the only one who has a teddy bear.

Discussion Questions

1. How would the story have been different if Reggie did not have a teddy bear?
2. Where did Reggie and Ira get the names for their teddy bears?
3. Why did Ira's sister make fun of Ira?
4. If you spent the night at a friend's house, what would you do for fun?

Activities (Please select one or more activities.)

1. Have your child create bear collages using pictures of bears from old magazines.
2. Have your child write or narrate a story from the perspective of Tah Tah, who perhaps felt neglected.
3. Have your child pretend that he or she is a reporter for a local television station. Ask your child to write a series of questions to ask Ira. Play the role of Ira and respond to your child's questions.
4. Talk with your child about favorite bedtime routines (e.g., watching television, taking a bath, putting on pajamas, saying goodnight, etc.). Make a list of bedtime routines and hang it in your child's room.
5. Have your child write an invitation to Ira to spend the night at your house, including all the activities planned.

Related Children's Books

A Bear Called Paddington by Michael Bond
Bears in Pairs by Niki Yektai
Jake and Rosie by Patricia Lillie
Jamaica's Find by Juanita Havill
Mr. Bear's Chair by Thomas Graham
Not This Bear! by Bernice Myers
Paddington's Storybook by Michael Bond

38

Island of the Blue Dolphins

Scott O'Dell
New York: Dell, 1960

Story Summary

This is the story of Karana, who finds herself alone after her tribe abandons their island to seek a safer world. Karana faces many trials and tribulations as she learns to survive on her own.

Discussion Questions

1. Would you want to live alone on an island for 10 years? Could you survive?

2. Which of Karana's personal traits helped her survive? Explain.

3. How did Karana feel after she was taken from the Island of the Blue Dolphins to a country where her language was not understood?

4. Could you survive on an island without modern technology (lights, television, cars)? Would you be content?

Activities (Please select one or more activities.)

1. Ask your child to draw a picture of the Island of the Blue Dolphins as he or she pictures it after reading the story. How does the illustration compare to other islands with which your child may be familiar?

2. Have your child construct a three-dimensional model of the house and yard Karana built for herself after her tribe left the island. Provide your child with a large piece of cardboard to use as a base; several boxes of toothpicks or Popsicle sticks to use in constructing the house and the fence; and paint, small rocks, sand, and miniature trees and bushes (available at hobby stores). Display the model in a prominent place.

3. Ask your child to list five items he or she would want to have if shipwrecked alone on an island. What items would your child consider to be most crucial for survival? Have your child interview family members and make a list of the five items desired by each person. Discuss similarities and differences among the lists.

4. Karana had a secret name that meant "the girl with the long brown hair." Have your child make up a secret name for each member of the family, based on a personal trait or physical characteristic.

Related Children's Books

Dolphins at Grassy Key by Marcia Seligson
Julie of the Wolves by Jean Craighead George
Sea Otter Rescue by Roland Smith
Whales by Seymour Simon

39

Jack and the Beanstalk

Lorinda Bryan Cauley
New York: Putnam's, 1983

Story Summary

This is the classic story of Jack, a handful of magic beans, and a mean giant. In the end, good triumphs over evil, and Jack and his mother live happily ever after.

Discussion Questions

1. Was Jack right or wrong in taking the hen and the golden harp from the giant?

2. What would you do if you found a hen that lays golden eggs?

3. How would your family react if you came home with magic beans?

Activities (Please select one or more activities.)

1. Before reading this book to your child, ask him or her to look at the cover and guess what the book is about. Ask your child if he or she has heard this story. What does your child know about giants and magical things?

2. Help your child grow beanstalks. Obtain pole bean seeds from a nursery or garden center. Plant two or three seeds in each of several paper cups filled with potting soil. Water the cups and place them on a window ledge or in sunlight. Place a straight stick or ruler in each cup. Ask your child to measure and note growth of the beanstalks over a period of several days, and then over a period of several weeks. Discuss the rate of growth and the elements beans need to survive. You and your child may want to photograph the beans at different stages of their growth. Place the notes and photographs into a special scrapbook.

3. Ask your child to tell a new version of the story, from the giant's point of view. How does the giant feel about Jack taking his hen and his golden harp? Is there a way to tell the story so that *everyone* lives happily ever after?

Related Children's Books

The Giants Go Camping by Jane Yolen
The Giant's Toe by Brock Cole
Jack and the Wonder Beans by James Still
The Little Giant by Robert Kraus
Lucky and the Giant by Benjamin Elkin
The Magic Beans by Margaret Hillert

40

Jacob Have I Loved

Katherine Paterson
New York: Crowell, 1980

Story Summary

This is the story of Louise, who grows up on a tiny Chesapeake Bay island in the early 1940s. She reveals how her twin sister, Caroline, robbed her of everything—her hopes, her friends, her mother, and even her name. Eventually, Louise begins to discover her own identity.

Discussion Questions

1. How would you respond to Louise's decision to cancel Christmas? What would you want to say to her?

2. Think about the times when Louise felt proud of Caroline. At these times, how did Louise feel about herself?

3. How would the story be different if the main characters were boys?

4. The war greatly affected Louise's life. What major event has affected your life?

5. If you were Louise's and Caroline's parent, what would you have done to reduce the sibling rivalry?

6. What is meant by the expression "let fear grab you and swing you around by the tail"? Has this ever happened to you?

Activities (Please select one or more activities.)

1. Your child may wish to make a tabletop model of Rass Island. Use a small piece of plywood for the base. Form modeling clay on the board (in the shape of an island) and press sand into it to simulate the surface of the island. Invite your child to place small objects (e.g., houses, furniture, plastic figures) on the "island."

2. Obtain a sheet of blank newsprint from an art supply store. Have your child lay on the sheet while you trace an outline of his or her body on the paper. Ask your child to record selected events in his or her life on the outline. Cut around the outline and post it in your child's room. You may wish to construct outlines of other family members, each of whom can record important events in their respective outlines. Post all the outlines in a prominent place in the house.

3. Ask your child to create a poster or advertisement designed to sell Caroline's journal. Show your child examples of advertisements in various magazine and have your child select the design elements that would help sell the journal.

4. When the family takes a vacation, have your child keep a family journal or travelogue. Periodically discuss the journal entries.

Related Children's Books

Big World, Small World by Jeanne Titherington
The Diary of a Paper Boy by Jean Larrea
The Diary of Trilby Frost by Diane Glaser

The Not So Wicked Step Mother by Lizi Boyd
What Kind of Family Is This by Barbara Seuling

41

James and the Giant Peach

Roald Dahl
New York: Penguin, 1961

Story Summary

One day James gets a bag of magic crystals that will free him from life with his horrible aunts. In his excitement, James drops the bag, and the crystals are sucked into the ground around the old peach tree. Something magical begins to happen to a peach at the tip of the tree—something that will *truly* change his life.

Discussion Questions

1. Would you want to have Aunt Sponge and Aunt Spiker as your aunts? Why?

2. If you were to write a letter to Roald Dahl, what would you write?

3. What would you have done if the old man had given you the magic crystals?

4. What might have happened if the cloud men had caught the peach?

Activities (Please select one or more activities.)

1. Help your child collect as many creatures in the story as possible (e.g., centipede, spider, earthworm, glow worm). Your child may want to make a temporary terrarium in a large glass bottle (a clean mayonnaise jar with moist soil, twigs, and grass works well). Have your child observe the habits of the creatures over a period of five days (*Insects as Pets* by Paul Villiard is a useful guide for taking care of insects). After five days, release the creatures to their original environments.

2. Ask your child to think of creative ways to use the creatures in your home. For example, a glow worm could be used as a night light for reading. Have your child illustrate these uses in a "Creature Guidebook."

3. Your child may enjoy making peaches and cream:

Peaches and Cream

Large box (6 oz.) apricot gelatin
1 quart sliced peaches
Small tub (4 oz.) whipped topping
1 cup sugar

Make gelatin in an 8-by-8-inch pan. When set, cut into small cubes. Sprinkle sugar over the peaches. Fold whipped topping and peaches into cubed gelatin and chill.

Related Children's Books by Roald Dahl

The BFG
Charlie and the Chocolate Factory
Danny the Champion of the World

The Enormous Crocodile
The Fantastic Mr. Fox
The Wonderful Story of Henry Sugar

John Henry

Ezra Jack Keats
New York: Pantheon, 1965

Story Summary

John Henry is a mighty hero of American folklore. In a story of will and determination, and of a human against a machine, the "man who was born with a hammer in his hand" challenges a new steam drill to a contest of strength, stamina, and power.

Discussion Questions

1. If you were to challenge the steam drill to a contest, what tools would you have chosen? Why?

2. If you were the author of this story, would you change the ending? If so, how would you change it? If not, why?

3. Why did the author write that John Henry was born with a hammer in his hand?

4. What other tools would John Henry be able to use with the same skill as the hammer?

Activities (Please select one or more activities.)

1. Invite your child to create a daily schedule for John Henry. When did he wake up? What chores did he tend to in the morning, in the afternoon, at night? When did he rest? When did he eat? Your child may want to chart the activities as a daily timeline.

2. Invite your child to create a travel journal for John Henry. Ask your child to imagine that he or she is John Henry and to record his thoughts and observations about growing up, work, and trains.

3. Encourage your child to develop advertisements or video commercials for the "contest" between John Henry and the steam drill. What enticements, slogans, or testimonials can your child use to promote the competition? Your child may want to look at promotions used for sports events in newspapers or magazines for ideas.

4. Your child may enjoy cutting out pictures from several old magazines and creating a notebook of trains throughout U.S. history. Post a selected picture of a train from a certain time period at the top of a sheet of paper. List facts about that train and its contributions below the picture. Gather together several of these sheets to make a "Train Notebook."

Related Children's Books

All Aboard Trains by Mary Harding
John Henry by Corinne Waden
The Railroads by Leonard Everett Fisher
Trains by Ray Broekel
Trains by H. R. Sheffer
Trains and Railroad Stations by Howard Kanetzke

43

Johnny Appleseed

Steven Kellogg
New York: Morrow, 1988

Story Summary

John Chapman, better known as Johnny Appleseed, was a historical figure whose wilderness adventures became larger-than-life legends. Born in Massachusetts during the Revolutionary War, John headed west as soon as he was able. Along the way, he cleared land and planted orchards to supply apples to the settlers who would follow. When the settlers arrived, John befriended them, often giving away his trees. Soon he became known as Johnny Appleseed, and legends about him spread quickly.

Discussion Questions

1. Do you believe the stories about Johnny in the wilderness? Why?
2. Would you have enjoyed living the life of Johnny Appleseed?
3. Why did Johnny keep planting trees?
4. Why did Johnny always live by himself?

Activities (Please select one or more activities.)

1. Work with your child to make a list of all the foods made from apples (e.g., cider, sauce, dumplings, etc.). Encourage family members to add to the list. Can you and your child come up with a list of more than 50 items? More than 100?

2. You and your child may enjoy making applesauce:

Applesauce

One bag of Jonathon or all-purpose apples   Honey
   (approximately 12-15 apples)   Cinnamon
2½ cups water

Cut apples into sixths and place into large pot with water. Cover and cook over low heat for about 45 minutes or until tender. Let apples cool. With a wooden spoon, place some of the mixture into a strainer and press apples through the mesh. Add honey and a pinch of cinnamon to the mixture prior to serving (hot or cold).

3. Visit a grocery store with your child and obtain as many different varieties of apples as you can. Have your child make a list of the qualities of each variety. What differences or similarities are there among all varieties of apples?

4. Obtain a map of the United States. Work with your child to calculate the distances Johnny traveled (e.g., Longmeadow, Massachusetts to Franklin, Pennsylvania; Ohio to Fort Wayne, Indiana). Talk with your child about the different routes and methods of travel he may have used.

Related Children's Books

The Apple and Other Fruits by Millicent Selsam
Folk Tales of Latin America by Shirlee Newman
Folk Tales of North America by Jean Corcoran

Johnny Tremain by Esther Forbes
Paul Bunyan by Steven Kellogg
Revolutionary War Weapons by C. B. Collry

Joyful Noise: Poems for Two Voices

Paul Fleischman
New York: Harper & Row, 1988

Story Summary

This is a creative and imaginative collection of poetry revolving around the "noises" of various insects. Each poem is designed so that the lines can be read by two people, together or alternately. Rhythmic descriptions of the movements and sounds of the insect world are heightened by the mental images conveyed by the words. This is a great "sharing" book for parents and children to enjoy together.

Discussion Questions

1. Which poems made you feel happy?

2. Which poems provided you with new insights or information about a specific insect?

3. Which poem would you want to read with a friend? What makes your selection particularly appropriate for two readers?

4. How do the poems in this book compare to the poems you have read in other books?

Activities (Please select one or more activities.)

1. Read selected poems together with your child. Encourage your child to share these poems with the family (perhaps present a poem at a special gathering or celebration).

2. Invite your child to select one of the insects from the book. Have your child list all the words the author uses to describe the insect. Have your child look in a book about nature or insects for other words to describe the insect. Which words are most poetic?

3. You and your child may want to create your own "poems for two voices" using the format of the author. Is there a special animal, plant, or location that could be described in poetic form?

4. Read other books of insect poems (see below) to your child. Invite your child to create his or her own illustrations for favorite poems. Discuss similarities and differences between this poetry and the poetry in *Joyful Noise*.

Related Children's Books

Bugs by Mary Ann Hoberman
Flit, Flutter, Fly! Poems About Bugs and Other Crawly Creatures by Lee Bennett Hopkins
The Hornbeam Tree and Other Poems by Charles Norman
Turtle in July by Marilyn Singer

45

Knots on a Counting Rope

Bill Martin Jr. and John Archambault
New York: Holt, 1987

Story Summary

This is the story of a blind boy who learns that he can overcome darkness with courage. He hears the story of his birth from his grandfather—a tale of two magnificent blue horses that give him the strength to live. The boy's horse becomes his eyes and they compete in an important race.

Discussion Questions

1. What do you know about the time you were born?

2. What things would you have to do differently if you were blind?

3. What is the bravest or most courageous thing you have ever done?

Activities (Please select one or more activities.)

1. You and your child may enjoy making Native American griddle cakes:

Griddle Cakes

2 cups Indian cornmeal
1 cup flour
1 tablespoon dark molasses

1 teaspoon baking soda
Buttermilk or sour milk

Mix together cornmeal, flour, molasses, and baking soda. Add enough buttermilk or sour milk to make a stiff batter. Drop by spoonfuls onto a hot griddle. Serve with butter and maple syrup.

2. You and your child may enjoy making a seed mosaic. Provide your child with different types of dried seeds or beans of various colors and sizes. Trace an outline of an illustration from the book onto a sheet of cardboard. Place white glue along the lines of the outline. Place beans and seeds along the glue lines (colored yarn and sequins can also be used for decorative effect). Put the mosaic in a special place.

3. Your child may want to make a Native American vest from a large paper grocery bag. Turn the bag upside down and cut directly up the middle on one wide side of the bag. Continue the cut two inches into the bottom of the bag. At the end of the straight cut, cut out a circle to make a neck hole. At this point, the bag may be turned inside out if there is advertising print on the outside. Cut arm holes into the sides of the bag. Cut four-inch slits around the bottom of the vest to make a fringe. Decorate the bag with Native American symbols using crayons or markers.

Related Children's Books

Annie and the Old One by Miska Miles
The Girl Who Loved Wild Horses by Paul Goble
Growing Up Indian by Evelyn Wolfson
Sheila Rae, the Brave by Kevin Henkes

The Silver Pony by Paul Goble
Stone Fox by John Reynolds Gardiner
Through Grandpa's Eyes by Patricia MacLachlan

The Legend of the Bluebonnet

Tomie dePaola
New York: Putnam, 1983

Story Summary

This is the story of the sacrifice made by a Comanche girl. She is the only one who can save her people from the ravages of a great drought. She gives up the thing most precious to her and in the end creates something far more beautiful.

Discussion Questions

1. What else could the Native Americans have done about the drought?
2. What might have happened if Lonely One had not sacrificed her doll?
3. Is Lonely One like anyone you know? Explain.
4. Why did all the others not want to sacrifice something?
5. What makes this such an enjoyable story?

Activities (Please select one or more activities.)

1. You and your child may want to study the effects of lack of water on plants. Provide your child with three potted flowers. Ask your child to water two of the flowers at the same time each day over a period of two or three weeks: one cup of water for the first flower and one-half cup of water for the second flower. Instruct your child not to water the third flower. Ask your child to note any changes in each of the flowers in a journal or notebook. Talk with your child about the need of all living things for water, and the consequences if a plant or animal does not receive sufficient water.

2. Work with your child to construct a tepee. Obtain several six-foot wooden dowels from a hobby store. Slant the poles so they meet at the top and securely tie the ends together with twine. Cover the structure with blank newsprint (available at hobby or art stores). Invite your child to paint symbols or pictures on the newsprint with tempera paint. If possible, set up the tepee in your child's room and invite him or her to use it as a reading area.

3. Visit a nursery or garden center and obtain some lupines (bluebonnets), or order them through a seed catalog. Plant several inside or outside your house. Put your child in charge of caring for the flowers.

Related Children's Books

American Indian Tales and Legends by Vladimoar Hulpach
Arrow to the Sun: A Pueblo Indian Tale by Gerald McDermott
Bluebonnets for Lucinda by Frances Sayers
Comanche by William Rollings
Indian Festivals by K. Brandt
Indians of the West by R. Bains
Wild Boy by Donald Clifford Snow

Leo the Late Bloomer

Robert Kraus
New York: Windmill, 1971

Story Summary

This is the story of Leo, a tiger who takes his time growing up. His parents are patient, and eventually he begins to bloom.

Discussion Questions

1. What makes Leo such an interesting character?
2. What does the term *late bloomer* mean to you?
3. How would you feel if you were a late bloomer?
4. If you were Leo's friend, how would you treat him?
5. If you were the author, would you change part of the story? Explain.

Activities (Please select one or more activities.)

1. Obtain a large sheet of newsprint (available at art and hobby stores). Have your child lie on the paper; trace his or her outline. Have your child cut out the outline. Invite your child to write (or dictate for you to write) words that best describe him or her. Place these words randomly within the outline. Hang the outline in your child's room. Encourage your child to add words to the outline periodically.

2. Your child may enjoy making casts of his or her feet or hands using flour dough:

Flour Dough

2 cups self-rising flour	2 tablespoons cooking oil
2 tablespoons alum	1 cup + 2 tablespoons
2 tablespoons salt	boiling water

Carefully mix together all ingredients and then knead into a dough. Roll out some of the mixture and have your child press a hand or foot into the mixture. Put the cast outside in the sun or bake in a slow oven (250 degrees) for several hours. Paint the cast.

After several months, your child may want to make additional casts to see his or her growth.

3. Have your child plant a bean or radish seed in a paper cup filled with potting soil. Discuss with your child how the seed will germinate and grow beneath the soil before a sprout can be seen above the soil. Have your child observe the cup and keep a journal on the growth of the seed. Have your child compare the hidden growth of the seed to the hidden growth of Leo.

Related Children's Books

All By Myself by Anna Grossnickle Hines
Bridget's Growing Day by Winifred Bromhall
The Growing Story by Ruth Krauss
Growing Up by Kevin Henkes

My Very First Book of Growth by Eric Carle
Next Year I'll Be Special by Patricia Reilly Giff
Something Special by David McPhail
You Are Much Too Small by Betty Boegehold

The Lion, the Witch, and the Wardrobe

C. S. Lewis
New York: Macmillan, 1950

Story Summary

In a mysterious and magical tale, four children travel to the world of Narnia through a wardrobe in an abandoned room of a big house. The children, together with the creatures of Narnia, help Aslan, a magnificent lion, battle and finally defeat a wicked witch.

Discussion Questions

1. Would you want to have a wardrobe like this in your house?

2. Why did the author choose a lion to represent good?

3. Would you change Narnia if you were King or Queen? Explain.

4. If you were Edmund, would you have gone to the side of the witch? Explain.

Activities (Please select one or more activities.)

1. Discuss with your child how he or she would feel about having to live in a land where it was always winter. What would be similar to or different from where you currently live? What might be some of the advantages and disadvantages?

2. Encourage your child to imagine that there is a magical wardrobe in his or her room. Invite your child to write a story (or make daily entries in a journal) about one or several adventures he or she takes through the wardrobe. Have your child share his or her adventures with other family members.

3. Visit a public library with your child and locate reference materials on the history of kings and queens. Your child may want to select one ruler to research extensively, or to investigate several famous kings and queens from the past. Have your child assemble a small booklet to share with the family.

Related Children's Books

Door in the Wall by Marguerite DeAngeli
The Last Battle by C. S. Lewis
The Ordinary Princess by M. M. Kaye
Prince Caspian by C. S. Lewis
R, My Name Is Rosie by Barbara Cohen
Witch of Blackbird Pond by Elizabeth George Speare

49

Lon Po Po

Ed Young
New York: Philomel, 1989

Story Summary

A woman lived with her three daughters in the countryside of northern China. One day she had to leave to visit their granny, so she warned her children not to open the door or let anyone in. Soon after her departure a wolf visits the house in the disguise of the grandmother. With wit and wisdom, the three children get the wolf to leave. This is a marvelously illustrated Chinese version of the classic tale *Little Red Riding Hood*.

Discussion Questions

1. What are the similarities between this story and the story *Little Red Riding Hood*? What are the differences?

2. Did you know before the end of the story what was going to happen to the wolf? Explain.

3. Were the three girls clever? Did they say or do anything that made you believe that they were wise?

4. The illustrations are done in a Chinese style of painting. What did you enjoy most about them? How do they differ from illustrations in other books you have read?

Activities (Please select one or more activities.)

1. Invite your child to retell the story from the perspective of the wolf, including his thoughts and observations. How would the wolf's version of the story be different than the version told by the author, or a version told by one of the three daughters?

2. Part of the story concerns ginkgo nuts. Though they are not commonly available in most grocery stores, you and your child may want to obtain other nuts (e.g., walnuts, cashews, pecans, Brazil nuts, etc.). Invite your child to rate the nuts according to taste.

3. Visit a public or school library with your child and obtain a copy of Ed Young's book *Yeh-Shen: A Cinderella Story from China*. Discuss similarities and differences between Young's version and the version with which your child is most familiar. Discuss similarities and differences between *Yen-Shen* and *Lon Po Po*.

4. You and your child may want to create a wall mural recounting important scenes from the story. Obtain a large sheet of newsprint from a hobby or art store. Use tempera paint to illustrate the scenes. Display the mural for the family to enjoy.

Related Children's Books

Bitter Bananas by Ed Young
Somewhere Today by Bert Kitchen
The True Story of the 3 Little Pigs by A. Wolf by Jon Scieszka
Wolves by John Wexo
Yeh-Shen: A Cinderella Story from China by Ed Young

50

Look!

April Wilson
New York: Dial, 1990

Story Summary

Each two-page spread in this wordless picture book consists of two seemingly identical illustrations. Closer inspection of each pair will reveal 12 vital differences. The differences are all revealed in the back of the book along with a fascinating guide to the wonders of nature.

Discussion Questions

1. Which of the 12 pairs of pictures gave you the most trouble?

2. How do animals camouflage themselves?

3. Which of the illustrations were most interesting to you?

Activities (Please select one or more activities.)

1. Invite your child to select one or more of the related titles listed below. Have your child make a list of the animals in the book that use camouflage. How many of these animals are insects? Mammals? Fish? What are some unusual ways that animals use camouflage?

2. Invite your child to obtain several different photographs of a family member. Have your child note the physical differences between any two photographs (e.g., hair style, height, etc.). Do children exhibit more differences than adults? Why?

3. As a follow-up activity, provide your child with April Wilson's *Look Again!* (New York: Dial, 1992). Post a wall map and encourage your child to plot the location of each two-page spread (from *Look!* and *Look Again!*) on the map. Write the name of the geographic location on an index card and tape it to the wall around the perimeter of the map.

Related Children's Books

Amazing Tropical Birds by Gerald Legg
Animal Camouflage: A Closer Look by Joyce Powzyk
Animal Camouflage: Hide-and-Seek Animals by Janet McDonnell
Chameleons: Dragons in the Trees by James Martin
Clever Camouflagers by Anthony D. Fredericks
Nature by Design by Bruce Brooks

51

Make Way for Ducklings

Robert McCloskey
New York: Viking, 1969

Story Summary

This is the story of Mr. and Mrs. Mallard Duck, who are looking for just the right place to raise their ducklings. After searching the country and city, they decide to settle on a nice quiet island.

Discussion Questions

1. What safe place would you choose for a duck family?

2. Why would the woods be a dangerous place for ducklings?

3. If you were a police officer, how would you help the ducks?

4. How would this story be different if the main characters were pigs instead of ducks?

Activities (Please select one or more activities.)

1. Encourage your child to make a poster of rules for raising ducklings. What procedures would people have to follow to ensure the safety of ducklings?

2. Your child may enjoy creating puppets of some of the characters in the story (e.g., policeman, ducks, drivers, etc.). Have your child draw illustrations of selected characters on cardboard, cut out the figures, and glue each to a Popsicle stick. Have your child enact a play using the puppets.

3. Invite your child to select one of the eight ducklings and write a biography of the duck's adult life, including such details as where the duck decides to move, whether the duck decides to get married, and so on.

4. Help your child locate Boston on a map of the United States or world. Ask your child to think of reasons why the mallards may have been flying over Boston. Discuss why ducks fly south in the winter and north in the spring.

5. Ask your child to make up names and create birth announcements for the eight ducklings.

Related Children's Books

The Duck with Squeaky Feet by Denys Cazet
Duckling Sees by Hargrave Hands
Happy Birthday, Dear Duck by Eve Bunting
Q Is for Duck by Mary Elting
Quack? by Mischa Richter

Miss Nelson Is Missing!

Harry Allard
Boston: Houghton Mifflin, 1977

Story Summary

This is the story of the students of Room 207, who are the most misbehaved students in school. When Miss Nelson, their teacher, suddenly disappears and Miss Viola Swamp arrives with hours of homework, the class tries to discover what has become of Miss Nelson.

Discussion Questions

1. Have you had a substitute similar to Miss Swamp? How was your substitute different?

2. Would you want to have Miss Nelson as a teacher?

3. How would you feel about having a substitute teacher like Viola Swamp?

4. If you were Detective McSmogg, where would you have looked for Miss Nelson? Why?

5. If you were one of the students, how would you have felt when Miss Nelson returned? Why?

Activities (Please select one or more activities.)

1. Have your child make a "Wanted" poster for Miss Nelson. What kind of information should be included on the poster? Hang the poster on the door of the refrigerator.

2. Discuss with your child the qualities of a good teacher. How should a good teacher treat students? How should a good teacher teach?

3. Have your child dictate or write a sequel to the story in which Detective McSmogg must find Miss Viola Swamp. Where would he look? Would he ever find her?

4. Your child might enjoy the two sequels to this story, *Miss Nelson Is Back* and *Miss Nelson Has a Field Day,* by Harry Allard.

5. Have your child look through old magazines and cut out pictures of children he or she would want to have in an ideal class. Have your child paste these pictures on a large sheet of paper. Discuss why the selected children would make an ideal class.

6. Have your child write a letter to Miss Nelson asking her to come back to the classroom. What could your child write that might convince Miss Nelson to return?

Related Children's Books

The Case of the Cat's Meow by Crosby Bonsall
Encyclopedia Brown by Donald Sobol (first title in a series)
The Homework Caper by Joan Lexaw
Something Queer Is Going On by Elizabeth Levy (first title in a series)

53

Miss Rumphius

Barbara Cooney
New York: Viking Penguin, 1982

Story Summary

This is the story of Alice Rumphius, who, like her grandfather, longs to travel around the world and live by the sea. Her grandfather advises her that she must also do one other thing—make the world a more beautiful place.

Discussion Questions

1. Would you want to have Miss Rumphius as a relative? Why?
2. How is Miss Rumphius an interesting character?
3. How is Miss Rumphius different from the elderly people that you know?
4. What kinds of adventures away from home would you want to experience?
5. Where would you want to live when you retire? What makes this place special to you?

Activities (Please select one or more activities.)

1. Invite your child to make a collage or poster of one of the countries mentioned in the book (e.g., Switzerland, Kenya, Morocco, Tahiti, Australia, or any country with kangaroos, mountains, deserts, a tropical environment, or lions).
2. Encourage your child to make an audio recording of the book and loan it to the school library. Include sound effects (e.g., lions roaring, waves on a shore, winter winds).
3. Provide your child with several types of flower seeds, including lupines. Have your child grow the seeds (outside, or indoors using a "grow lamp"). Invite your child to chart the germination rates of the seeds as well as differences in the shape, color, and size of the flowers. How are lupines different from other flowers?
4. Invite your child to look through the local phone book and compile a list of services for elderly people (e.g., nursing homes, special equipment, social groups, etc.).

Related Children's Books

The Little Island by Golden MacDonald
Now One Foot, Now the Other by Tomie dePaola
The Voyage of the Ludgate Hill by Nancy Willard

Missing May

Cynthia Rylant
New York: Orchard, 1992

Story Summary

This is a touching story about an old man, a young girl, and a strange boy and how they form a unique and meaningful relationship after the death of the old man's wife, May. They set out on a journey to look for some sign from May and to learn about life and the meaning given to it by special people in their lives. *Missing May* won the Newbery Award in 1993.

Discussion Questions

1. Are any of the characters in this story similar to your relatives or friends?

2. Why did the author include Cletus as a major character?

3. What did the author mean at the end of the book by the words "a big wind came and set everything free."

4. What lessons did you learn from reading this book?

5. If you had a chance to talk with Ob, what would you say to him?

Activities (Please select one or more activities.)

1. Have your child talk with grandparents or senior citizens about life in "the good old days." You and your child may want to visit a senior center and interview individuals about their memories and recollections of life. Your child may want to make an audio recording of these interviews.

2. Discuss with your child the ways that people honor and remember those who have died. Are there special customs or traditions within your family, ethnic group, or religion that celebrate those who have died? Discuss any customs and the reasons why these customs are practiced.

3. Invite your child to write a fictitious letter to Ob. What could your child write to comfort him? What "words of wisdom" could he or she share? Your child may want to make a special sympathy card for Ob using examples available from a card shop.

4. Your child may want to write a letter to Cynthia Rylant commenting on this book. Ms. Rylant can be addressed in care of her publisher (Orchard Books, 95 Madison Avenue, New York, NY 10016). Advise your child that he or she may not receive a personal reply because Ms. Rylant receives so many letters that she cannot reply to all of them herself.

Related Children's Books

A Blue-Eyed Daisy by Cynthia Rylant
A Fine White Dust by Cynthia Rylant
On My Honor by Marion Bauer
Shiloh by Phyllis Naylor
The Winter Room by Gary Paulsen

55

The Mitten

Alvin Tresselt
New York: Scholastic, 1964

Story Summary

This is the story of a boy who goes into the woods to gather wood for his grandmother. When he loses a mitten, the animals of the forest decide to crawl inside to keep warm.

Discussion Questions

1. Would the story have been different if the boy had lost two mittens? Explain.
2. Would the story have been different if the bear had been the first animal inside the mitten? Explain.
3. Would the story have been different if the boy had been walking through a city?
4. What animal in the story would you want to be? Why?

Activities (Please select one or more activities.)

1. Work with your child to make a garment like the bear's vest from a large paper grocery bag. Cut out a head hole and two arm holes. Ask your child to decorate the vest. Have your child wear the vest as you retell the story.

2. Provide your child with a piece of blue construction paper, a bag of white cotton balls (for snow), glue, crayons, and markers. Have your child make a "snowy" picture, including trees, animals, and an illustration of the boy.

3. Provide your child with several old magazines, catalogs, and calendars. Ask your child to cut out pictures depicting the four seasons and glue one picture on each of four large index cards. Have your child arrange the cards in order and post them on the door of the refrigerator.

4. Your child may enjoy making a construction paper snowflake. Have your child cut out a large circle from a sheet of construction paper. Fold the circle in half, and fold again in thirds. Have your child cut designs along all edges of the pie-shaped piece. Unfold the paper and invite your child to retell the story from the snowflake's point of view.

5. Obtain an old sheet or blanket. Ask your child to pretend that the sheet or blanket is a giant mitten. Have your child pretend to be one of the animals as you retell the story.

Related Children's Books

First Snow by Emily Arnold McCully
The First Snowfall by Anne Rockwell and Harlow Rockwell
Our Snowman by M. B. Goffstein
Sadie and the Snowman by Allen Morgan
Snow Lion by David McPhail
The Snowman Who Went for a Walk by Mira Lobe
The Snowy Day by Ezra Jack Keats
Something Is Going to Happen by Charlotte Zolotow

Mrs. Frisby and the Rats of NIMH

Robert C. O'Brien

New York: Atheneum, 1971

Story Summary

This is the story of Mrs. Frisby, a widowed mouse who must find a way to rescue her sickly son. Her last hope takes her to the Rats of NIMH, a group of rodents with human brilliance. The rats devise a plan that will save Mrs. Frisby, her son, and themselves, from destruction.

Discussion Questions

1. What would happen if rats ruled the world?
2. What helped the rats continue to gain knowledge?
3. What might have happened if the rats had been caught by NIMH?
4. Would you want to have NIMH rats living near your house? Why?
5. Do you think that Mrs. Frisby or her children ever saw the rats again?

Activities (Please select one or more activities.)

1. Your child may enjoy conducting library research on owls. What habits and habitats of owls are unusual? How do owls differ from other birds?
2. Encourage your child to make a chart that compares the Rats of NIMH to common household rodents. What are the similarities and differences?
3. Help your child create a dictionary of "rodent-related" words and phrases. Included might be "rat race," "quiet as a mouse," and "RATS!" Have your child compile as many terms as possible and design an appropriate "dictionary" for other children.
4. Obtain papier-mâché from a local hobby store. Work with your child to create a replica of the rat village as described in the book. Use poster or tempera paint to color the village. Display the model village on the family bookcase.

Related Children's Books

Abel's Island by William Steig
Basil of Baker Street by Eve Titus
Ben and Me by Robert Lawson
The Cricket in Times Square by George Seldon
The Great Rescue Operation by Jean Van Leeuwen
Stuart Little by E. B. White

57

Mufaro's Beautiful Daughters

John Steptoe
New York: Lothrop, Lee & Shepard, 1987

Story Summary

This is the story of Mufaro and his two beautiful daughters, Nyasha and Manyara, who live in a small village in Africa. Nyasha is kind and considerate, while Manyara is selfish and spoiled. When the king announces that he is looking for the most beautiful woman in the land to be his wife, Manyara is determined to reach the city before her sister. In the end, kindness prevails over greed.

Discussion Questions

1. How is the daily life in the village in this story different from your daily life? How is it similar?
2. Could this story take place in today's world? Why?
3. Why did Manyara dislike her sister? What did Nyasha feel for Manyara?
4. If you could speak with one of the characters in the story, which one would you choose, and what would you say?
5. Would you want to live in Africa? Why?

Activities (Please select one or more activities.)

1. Read the introductory page of the story to your child, explaining the meanings of the names of the characters. Discuss with your child the meaning of his or her name (name dictionaries are available in libraries and bookstores). Have your child write his or her name on a sheet of construction paper, decorate it with pictures of things he or she likes to do, and post it in a special place.

2. Have your child create puppets of the story characters by decorating old socks with markers, colored paper, bits of yarn, scraps of fabric, and glue. Paint several story scenes on butcher paper or an old bed sheet. Hang the background on a bulletin board and use a table turned on its side as a stage for the puppet theater. With your child, reenact portions of the story for the family. Consult *Children's Crafts* (San Francisco, CA: Sunset Books, 1976) for puppetry ideas.

3. Obtain a copy of the book *Why Mosquitoes Buzz in People's Ears* by Verna Aardema (New York: Dial, 1975). Explain to your child that this is an African folktale as is *Mufaro's Beautiful Daughters*. Ask your child to compare the two stories. Invite your child to create a folktale to explain something in his or her life or to explain a characteristic of a particular creature.

Related Children's Books

African Animals by John Wallace Purcell
Art and Life in Africa by Christopher D. Roy
Ashanti to Zulu: African Traditions by Margaret Musgrove
Bringing the Rain to Kapiti Plain by Verna Aardema
Count on Your Fingers, African Style by Claudia Zaslavsky
In Africa by Marc Bernheim and Evelyne Bernheim
Why Mosquitoes Buzz in People's Ears by Verna Aardema

The Napping House

Audrey Wood

San Diego: Harcourt Brace Jovanovich, 1984

Story Summary

The author uses cumulative rhyme to tell the story of a sleeping granny and the host of others who join her for a nap. One individual after another joins the pile, until the humorously disastrous ending.

Discussion Questions

1. Would you want to nap with so many individuals? Would it be fun? Why?

2. Do you have a favorite stuffed animal or pet you like to sleep with?

3. What do you like to do on a dreary, rainy day? Who do you like to be with?

Activities (Please select one or more activities.)

1. Before reading the book, ask your child what he or she thinks it is about (according to the title). Write down your child's predictions and discuss them after you have shared the story.

2. Discuss with your child the funniest, the scariest, the darkest, or the noisiest place he or she has ever slept. Where is the most comfortable place your child has slept?

3. You and your child may want to make puppets using old socks, pieces of cloth, yarn, glue, and buttons or sequins (for eyes, mouth, buttons on a shirt, etc.). Retell the story, providing opportunities for your child to "pile" the puppets on top of each other as in the book.

4. Talk with your child about babies' and toddlers' need for naps and what happens when they do not nap. Why is it important for growing babies to get lots of sleep?

Related Children's Books

I Know an Old Lady by Rose Bonne
Moonflute by Audrey Wood
The Nap Master by William Kotzwinkle
Naptime by Gylbert Coker

59

The New Kid on the Block

Jack Prelutsky
New York: Greenwillow, 1984

Story Summary

A "must have" book for any family library, this rollicking collection of 107 poems written just for a child's funny bone is filled with lots of laughs and loads of giggles. Poems range from a child's encounters with other children to body parts.

Discussion Questions

1. Which poems did you most enjoy? Which poem made you laugh the most?

2. Which poem was most like your life or a specific event in your life?

3. Which poems would you enjoy sharing with your friends? Explain.

Activities (Please select one or more activities.)

1. Read to your child some of the poems about body parts (i.e., "Be Glad Your Nose Is on Your Face," "I've Got an Itch," "You Need to Have an Iron Rear," "Baloney Belly Billy"). Invite your child to select a specific body part (e.g., ear, tongue, kneecap, toe) and create a poem similar in style to one of the poems in the book.

2. Invite your child to separate some of the poems into specific categories of his or her own choosing (e.g., "Creature Poems," "Family Poems," "Eating Poems"). Encourage your child to designate each day of the week as a day for sharing a specific category of poems.

3. Have your child invite family and friends to record audio versions of selected poems. Your child can listen to cassettes of his or her favorite "DJs" reading poetry.

Related Children's Books

The Baby Uggs Are Hatching by Jack Prelutsky
Falling Up by Shel Silverstein
A Light in the Attic by Shel Silverstein
The Random House Book of Poetry for Children by Jack Prelutsky
Tyrannosaurus Was a Beast by Jack Prelutsky
Where the Sidewalk Ends by Shel Silverstein

60

One Small Square: Cactus Desert

Donald M. Silver
New York: W. H. Freeman, 1995

Story Summary

This terrific "hands-on" book introduces young scientists to many of the plants and animals that inhabit the desert. The author and illustrator skillfully guide youngsters through explorations of this incredible environment with scientific information and hints for real-life observation.

Discussion Questions

1. What was the most interesting discovery you made while reading this book?

2. Which animals would you want to learn more about? Which plants would you want to learn more about?

3. What do you now know about deserts that you did not know before?

4. What makes a desert distinctive?

5. Would you enjoy living in a desert? Explain.

Activities (Please select one or more activities.)

1. Check out or rent a video about the desert to watch with your child (many libraries and video stores have a variety of nature videos). Invite your child to watch for the plants and animals described in the book.

2. Encourage your child to make two lists: one of the features and characteristics of animals that help them survive in the desert (e.g., eat at night, hide in shade, etc.) and another of the features of plants that help them survive in the desert (e.g., spines, waxy coating, etc.).

3. Your child may enjoy reading other books in this series, including *Backyard*, *Seashore*, *Cave*, *African Savanna*, *Arctic Tundra*, and *Pond* (New York: W. H. Freeman).

4. Visit a local nursery or gardening center with your child. Look at the variety of cactus plants available and discuss their similarities. Purchase a plant and encourage your child to care for it.

Related Children's Books

America's Deserts by Marianne Wallace
Cactus Hotel by Brenda Guiberson
Desert by Ron Hirschi
The Desert Is Theirs by Byrd Baylor
Desert Voices by Byrd Baylor
A Desert Year by Carol Lerner
Mojave by Diane Siebert
This Place Is Dry by Vicki Cobb

61

Ox-Cart Man

Donald Hall
New York: Viking, 1979

Story Summary

This is the story of an ox-cart man, who in the fall packs his cart with wool, mittens, candles, linen, shingles, brooms, and all the things he and his family have made during the past year. He sets off for Portsmouth Market, where he sells everything, including the ox and the cart. Upon returning home, he and his family begin anew—making candles, whittling brooms, carving a yoke—preparing for the next fall.

Discussion Questions

1. Do you have chores or jobs similar to those of the children in this story?

2. Do you have in your home any of the items made by the ox-cart man's family? How were the items in your home manufactured?

3. Would you want to live in eighteenth-century New England? What difficulties would you experience? What would you most enjoy?

4. How is your family similar to the family in this story? How is your family different?

Activities (Please select one or more activities.)

1. Invite your child to create a model of an ox cart using oatmeal boxes cut in half lengthwise, rubber wheels, wire, and pieces of fabric.

2. Encourage your child to create an original "advertisement" for some of the goods the ox-cart man was to sell in Portsmouth. What modern-day advertising techniques should be included in the advertisement to ensure a sale?

3. Your child may enjoy making candles as portrayed in the story. Obtain paraffin (available at hobby stores), half-pint milk cartons, old crayons, paper clips, pencils, a double boiler, and wicks (available at hobby stores). For each candle, tie a paper clip (for weight) to a wick. Tie the other end of the wick to the middle of a pencil and lay the pencil across the top of a half-pint milk carton (make sure the wick hangs down in the center of the carton). Put paraffin and crayon shavings (for color) into the top of a double boiler. Fill the bottom of the double boiler with water and boil. When the paraffin has melted, carefully and slowly pour the liquid into the milk carton, filling it almost to the top. When the paraffin has cooled, peel off the milk carton.

Related Children's Books

A Circle of Seasons by Myra Livingston
Sarah Morton's Day: A Day in the Life of a Pilgrim Girl by Kate Waters
The Strength of the Hills: A Portrait of a Family Farm by Nancy P. Graff

62

The Paper Bag Princess

Robert Munsch
Toronto: Annick, 1980

Story Summary

This is the story of Elizabeth, a beautiful princess who intends to marry a prince named Ronald. Unfortunately, a dragon destroys her castle and captures Ronald, leaving Elizabeth with only a paper bag for clothing. Elizabeth decides to rescue her beloved Ronald—but after a series of imaginative escapades with the dragon, she makes a startling discovery. A hilarious retelling of classic "dragon tales" that will have youngsters begging for more books by this whimsical and creative author.

Discussion Questions

1. Did the ending of this story surprise you? Explain.

2. How is this story different from other stories about "knights in shining armor" and "fearsome dragons"?

3. Do you think Elizabeth was smart? What events led you to believe so?

4. Who would you most want to have as a friend: Elizabeth, Ronald, or the dragon? Why?

Activities (Please select one or more activities.)

1. Obtain other books by Robert Munsch (see below) for your child. Discuss with your child reasons why this author is one of the most well-known and popular authors in Canada. What does Mr. Munsch include in his books that makes them so enjoyable and funny?

2. Invite your child to play the role of an advice columnist. Encourage your child to write a letter of advice to Ronald. What "words of wisdom" could your child impart to Ronald? Your child may want to offer some advice to the dragon as well.

3. Introduce your child to legends about dragons, castles, "knights in shining armor" (e.g., King Arthur and the Knights of the Round Table), and princes and princesses. Have your child visit a library to find collections of stories and folktales.

4. Invite your child to create articles of clothing using large paper grocery bags. Have your child construct a paper bag dress, a paper bag shirt or vest, or paper bag pants using scissors, glue, and staples. What are the difficulties encountered in making paper bag clothes?

Related Children's Books by Robert Munsch

I Have to Go!
Millicent and the Wind
Moira's Birthday

Pigs
Show and Tell
Thomas' Snowsuit

63

Paul Bunyan

Steven Kellogg
New York: Holt, 1984

Story Summary

This is the story of a giant man named Paul Bunyan. Paul grows up in the family business of logging. He loves working as a lumberjack and one day starts his own business.

Discussion Questions

1. What would it be like to be bigger and stronger than any person alive?

2. How would it feel to be trapped somewhere, unable to share your birthday and holidays with your family and friends?

3. What would you have done if you were one of Paul Bunyan's parents?

4. How would it feel to travel across the country by foot?

Activities (Please select one or more activities.)

1. Have your child draw a picture of Paul, making him something other than a lumberjack (e.g., doctor, dentist, cowboy, steel worker). Encourage your child to write a story about Paul Bunyan in his new occupation. What difficulties does he encounter? What adventures does he have?

2. Ask your child to create an "expense" list of all the damages Paul incurred during the course of the story. Your child may want to draw up a bill for all the damages listing each item damaged and its replacement value.

3. Provide your child with a list of the ingredients needed to make pancakes for 3 to 4 people (e.g., 2 cups pancake mix, $1\frac{1}{3}$ cups milk, and 1 egg makes about 18 dollar-sized pancakes). Challenge your child to calculate the amounts of ingredients that would be needed to serve 100 people.

4. Have your child create an informational brochure listing precautionary steps to take in the event of an approaching blizzard. What advice can your child suggest that could help others endure a blizzard?

Related Children's Books

The Giant's Toe by Brock Cole
Idle Jack by Autry Maitland
Journey Cake, Ho! by Ruth Sawyer
Ol' Paul the Mighty Logger by Glen Rounds
Pecos Bill by Steven Kellogg

64

The People Could Fly

Virginia Hamilton
New York: Knopf, 1985

Story Summary

This is a compilation of African folktales about everything from animals to people. Included are legends and myths of people who could fly, smart animals, slaves, and runaway slaves.

Discussion Questions

1. In *The People Could Fly*, what might have happened if the people had never lost their wings?

2. If you had lived a free life and were suddenly captured, how would you feel and what would you do?

3. How do animals communicate with each other?

4. Folktales are passed down from generation to generation. Are there any stories in our family that have been passed down to you?

Activities (Please select one or more activities.)

1. Work with your child to create a collage. Have your child collect a variety of photographs, magazine pictures, and hand-drawn pictures of animals found in Africa. Have your child assemble and paste these pictures onto a large sheet of construction paper. Hang the collage in a prominent location. Ask your child to select an animal from the collage and conduct library research on its habits and habitat. Invite your child to share one new fact about the selected animal each day.

2. Have your child select a story from the book. Discuss with your child reasons why this story is a good example of a folktale. What qualities ensure the longevity of the story? What folktales does your child know? Do all folktales have the same qualities? Why are some stories more memorable than others? Visit a storytelling group (check the phone book or a library), listen to the stories, and compare these stories to the stories in *The People Could Fly*.

3. Folktales are passed down from generation to generation. Families pass down other beloved items as well, including rings, dolls, and clothing. Discuss with your child any family heirlooms and why they have been passed down through the years. Have your child select one item of his or hers to pass down, and ask your child to explain the importance of this item to succeeding generations.

Related Children's Books

African Myths and Legends by Kathleen Arnott
An Anthology of Modern Black African and Black American Literature by William Henry Rolanson
Black Folk Tales by Julius Lester
Jump Ship to Freedom by James Collier and Christopher Collier
Roll of Thunder, Hear My Cry by Mildred Taylor

65

The Polar Express

Chris Van Allsburg
Boston: Houghton Mifflin, 1985

Story Summary

Late one Christmas Eve, a young boy is invited to board the Polar Express. The mysterious train takes the boy to the North Pole to meet Santa Claus, where he receives a special present.

Discussion Questions

1. Why did the boy's mother and father not hear the bell?

2. How do the illustrations in the book make you feel? How are these illustrations different from illustrations in other books you have read?

3. Why did the bell continue to ring for the boy, even though he was older?

4. Why did the boy lose the bell?

5. Is this a good book to share at Christmas? Can this book be read at other times during the year?

6. Why did the author write this book? What would you want to say to Chris Van Allsburg?

Activities (Please select one or more activities.)

1. Your child may enjoy making a whipped cream picture. Spread whipped cream (to represent snow) on a clean table top or large sheet of paper. Have your child use his or her fingers to copy illustrations from the book into the whipped cream.

2. Your child may want to write a letter to Chris Van Allsburg commenting on the book. Send the letter in care of Mr. Allsburg's publisher (Houghton Mifflin Company, 2 Park Street, Boston, MA 02108). Advise your child that he or she may not receive a personal reply because Mr. Allsburg receives so many letters that he cannot reply to all of them himself.

3. Your child may enjoy creating a Polar Express milk carton train. Obtain empty half-pint milk cartons, tempera paint, paintbrushes, liquid soap, scissors, and pipe cleaners. Mix dry tempera paint and liquid soap (the soap makes the paint stick to the waxy surface of the milk carton). Invite your child to paint the cartons various colors. Cut off the tops of the cartons, leaving open boxes. Holding the milk carton with the open side up, punch a hole into two opposite sides. Connect the train cars together with pipe cleaners, knotting the ends of the pipe cleaners inside the cartons. Have your child operate the Polar Express as you retell the story.

Related Children's Books

The Christmas Box by Eve Merriam
Christmas Eve by Susie Stevenson
The Christmas Party by Adrienne Adams

A Christmas Promise by Clark Carrier
Joy to Christmas by Beatrice Chute
Snow Before Christmas by Tasha Tudor

A River Ran Wild

Lynne Cherry
San Diego: Gulliver, 1992

Story Summary

This true story details the "life history" of the Nashua River in New England. This is a fascinating book about the people who lived along its banks; their customs, traditions, and culture; how their lives were shaped by the forces and resources of the river; and how people can "overpower" a natural resource.

Discussion Questions

1. Is the Nashua River similar to any river, stream, or water source near where you live?
2. Do you believe that people intentionally set out to pollute a river? Explain.
3. What should people do every day to prevent the pollution of streams and rivers?

Activities (Please select one or more activities.)

1. Invite your child to visit a nearby stream or river. Encourage your child to observe the water carefully. Does the water have an unusual smell or color? Is there any sign of pollution? If so, what might be the cause of this pollution? How might the community clean up the river?

2. Invite your child to write a letter to the editor of the local newspaper regarding the need to keep the environment clean. Encourage your child to explain the value of the local environment to future generations of children.

3. Invite your child to write The Isaak Walton League of America (1401 Wilson Boulevard, Level B, Arlington, VA 22209) and request a copy of their free "Save Our Streams" booklet and other information about pollution.

4. Discuss with your child the border illustrations on the left-hand pages throughout the book. How do these illustrations help the reader understand the setting and time period of this story? Why are specific items included in the illustrations?

Related Children's Books

50 Simple Things Kids Can Do to Save the Earth by John Javna
Our Endangered Planet: Groundwater by Mary Hoff
Our Endangered Planet: Rivers and Lakes by Mary Hoff
Simple Nature Experiments with Everyday Materials by Anthony D. Fredericks
Water Pollution by Darlene Stille

67

Round Trip

Ann Jonas
New York: Greenwillow, 1983

Story Summary

This delightful and inviting book for children records the sights on a one-day trip to the city with black-and-white illustrations. The story continues with the return trip home when the reader turns the book upside down and reads from the back to the front.

Discussion Questions

1. Which direction of the trip did you most enjoy?

2. What other places might have been included on the trip?

3. Which illustration was your favorite? Why?

Activities (Please select one or more activities.)

1. Work with your child to create a milk carton city. Obtain various sizes of milk cartons, paint and paintbrushes, construction paper, and glue. Arrange the milk cartons on a large sheet of construction paper. Glue down the milk cartons. Paint them in blacks and whites, following the illustrations in the story as examples. You may want to take photographs of the city from different angles. Develop the photographs and discuss with your child reasons why the city looks different depending on the perspective of the observer.

2. You and your child may want to make a rain gauge to measure rainfall over a period of several months. Obtain a glass jar about one inch in diameter (an olive jar works well), a plastic ruler, and rubber bands. Position the ruler vertically alongside the jar with rubber bands to hold it in place. Help your child record the amount of rainfall after each rain. Discuss the different amounts recorded and the reasons why rainfall varies.

3. You may want to use the following demonstration to help your child understand how plants obtain water: Fill a glass halfway with tap water. Add several drops of food coloring to the water. Cut off the end of a stalk of celery and put the celery stalk (cut end first) into the water. Have your child observe the celery stalk each hour for several hours. Explain to your child that this demonstration models a plant obtaining water from the soil.

Related Children's Books

Have You Seen Roads? by Joanne Oppenheim
The Lonely Skyscraper by Jenny Hawkes Worth
Once Around the Block by Kevin Henkes
Round the World by Ester Brain
What's in a Community by Caroline Arnold

Sadako and the Thousand Paper Cranes

Eleanor Coerr
New York: Putnam, 1977

Story Summary

This is the story of Sadako, who is two years old when the atom bomb is dropped on Hiroshima in 1945. Although she is not injured during the bombing, she becomes ill with leukemia 10 years later. A friend tells Sadako that if she folds 1,000 paper cranes, they will bring her good luck and she will live a long life. Sadako dies before she can fold all the cranes, but her classmates fold the remainder. The cranes are buried with Sadako.

Discussion Questions

1. How is Sadako similar to you or to any of your friends?

2. Why is the number 1,000 important?

3. What special things have you done for your friends? What special things have your friends done for you?

4. What is the most touching moment for you in this story? Explain.

Activities (Please select one or more activities.)

1. Obtain photocopies of major newspapers from 1945 reporting on the bombing and its effects (check a college library or newspaper company). Ask your child to use this information to write and record a "radio announcement" reporting on the event.

2. Ask your child to interview grandparents or elder friends about their lives at the time of the bombing, how the war changed their lives, and how they felt about the war and the bombing. Have your child share the information with the family.

3. You and your child may enjoy making this popular Japanese salad:

Black and White Salad

4–6 boiled potatoes	Dill
2 tablespoons white vinegar	Powdered mace
Lemon juice (½ lemon)	1 can cooked mussels
Salt and pepper	1 can button mushrooms
Fresh parsley	Walnut halves

Slice potatoes. Mix together vinegar, lemon juice, salt, pepper, and a large handful of parsley. Marinate the potatoes in this mixture. Add a pinch of dill and a pinch of powdered mace. Drain the mussels and the mushrooms. Fold gently into the potatoes. Garnish with walnut halves. Makes 4 servings.

Related Children's Books

The Crane Wife by Sumyko Yagawa
Hiroshima No Pika by Toshi Maiuki
I Had a Friend Named Peter: Talking to Children About the Death of a Friend by Janice Cohen

Learning to Say Good-bye by Eda LeShan
My Hiroshima by Junko Morimoto
We Live in Japan by Kazuhide Kawamata

69

The Salamander Room

Anne Mazer
New York: Knopf, 1991

Story Summary

A young boy discovers an orange salamander in the woods and takes it home. Prodded by a series of questions from his mother, he imagines all the ways he will care for his newfound friend, and how his companion will live.

Discussion Questions

1. What must one think about when caring for an animal?

2. If you could choose any animal in the world to have as a pet, what animal would you choose?

3. If you were to write a sequel to this story, what would happen?

Activities (Please select one or more activities.)

1. Contact a zoologist or herpetologist in the biology or zoology department of a local college or university. Make arrangements for your child to ask questions.

2. Invite your child to research other books on salamanders. Encourage your child to research the lifestyles and habits of different species of salamanders. Discuss the similarities and differences.

3. Invite your child to rewrite a portion of the story from the perspective of the salamander. What did the salamander observe and experience? How did the salamander view the boy? What did it think about living in the boy's bedroom?

Related Children's Books

Frogs, Toads, Lizards, and Salamanders by Nancy Parker and Joan Wright
Reptiles and Amphibians: Nature Stories for Children by Robert Wrigley
Snakes, Salamanders and Lizards by Diane Burns

Sarah, Plain and Tall

Patricia MacLachlan
New York: Harper & Row, 1985

Story Summary

This is the touching story of a father and his children who live alone on the prairie. After the father puts an advertisement in the newspaper, Sarah Wheaton comes to live with them for a month. Many lessons are learned as the month turns into forever.

Discussion Questions

1. Would you want to have Sarah as a mother if you were not with your real mother? Why?
2. What happened to the real mother?
3. If you could be any person in this story, who would you be? Why?
4. Why was singing such an important part of the story?
5. Would you enjoy living like the family in the book?

Activities (Please select one or more activities.)

1. Sarah came from Maine, a state with a turbulent seacoast. You and your child may enjoy making a wave bottle. Fill a soda bottle (one with a screw top) one-third full with salad oil. Fill the rest of the bottle with water (completely to the top). Add several drops of blue food coloring. Screw on the top tightly and gently rock the bottle back and forth on its side. Have your child note the action of the "waves" inside the bottle.

2. Your child may enjoy creating a model of his or her favorite character from the story. Use modeling clay (available at hobby stores), or make the following clay: Mix together 4 cups flour, 1 cup salt, and $1\frac{1}{2}$ cups warm water. Knead for approximately 10 minutes (the mixture should be stiff, yet pliable). Mold the clay into the desired shape, and allow it to air dry. Bake on a cookie sheet or aluminum foil in a slow oven (250 degrees) until completely dry. Paint the model with tempera paint.

3. Most of this story was written from the perspective of the children. Invite your child to rewrite a portion of the story from Papa's perspective. What would he see and say that would be different from what the children saw and heard?

Related Children's Books

Emma's Vacation by David McPhail
Ox-Cart Man by Donald Hall
Toby in the Country, Toby in the City by Maxine Bozzo
A Week of Raccoons by Gloria Whelan
Yonder by Tony Johnston

71

School Bus

Donald Crews
New York: Greenwillow, 1984

Story Summary

A school bus goes through its daily route, picking up passengers and taking them to school and then returning them home again.

Discussion Questions

1. If you ride a school bus, how do you feel?

2. How would you feel if you were a bus?

3. What are some different ways someone could get to school?

Activities (Please select one or more activities.)

1. Take a walk with your child through your neighborhood or community. Record the different types of transportation you see (cars, trucks, buses, airplanes, etc.). Record the different types of colors of these vehicles. Do certain forms of transportation use a particular color (e.g., taxicabs)? What form of transportation has the largest variety of colors?

2. Position several chairs at the center of the living room to represent the seats on a bus. Have your child pretend to be a bus driver while other members of the family pretend to be passengers. Ask your child to give directions to the passengers; "drive" the bus to specified locations, letting off passengers along the way, and return the bus to its garage.

3. Discuss with your child the rules that should be followed on a bus. Why is it necessary for passengers to be careful when riding on a bus? How do the safety rules for a bus differ from safety rules for a car?

4. Provide your child with an empty shoebox, yellow and black paint, and paintbrushes. Help your child paint the box to resemble a school bus. You and your child may want to make models of people from modeling clay (see page 72, activity 2 for a recipe for homemade clay) to place inside the bus (cut out windows if desired). Display the bus on the family bookcase.

Related Children's Books

By Camel or By Car by Guy Billout
How Does It Get There? by George Sullivan
How My Library Grew by Martha Alexander
Road Closed by Michael Kehoe

The Sign of the Beaver

Elizabeth George Speare
Boston: Houghton Mifflin, 1983

Story Summary

This is the story of a 12-year-old boy who, with the help of a Native American friend, grows up in a hurry. This wonderful story shows how two boys from different cultures can experience a rewarding friendship.

Discussion Questions

1. How would you feel if you had to stay alone in a cabin in the woods?

2. Would you want to live a lifestyle like that of Attean and his tribe?

3. If Matt did not have the two books, could he have taught Attean to read? Explain.

4. If you were Matt, would you have gone with the Native Americans?

5. If Attean were to move to a big city, could he adjust to the changes in lifestyle? What would Attean have trouble adjusting to?

6. What would Matt have done if his parents had never showed up?

7. How will Matt's parents react to his stories about Attean?

Activities (Please select one or more activities.)

1. Ask your child to imagine that he or she will be going into the wilderness to establish a home. The cabin is already built, but it is empty. Your child may take only 20 items. Discuss with your child the 20 items that should be taken. What items are more crucial to survival in the wilderness than others? Does it make a difference if your child does not know how long he or she will be in the wilderness?

2. Encourage your child to create an imaginary newspaper based on the characters and events of this story. Ask your child to invent several headlines for the newspaper based on events in the book (e.g., "Matt Meets Indians," "Young Boy Alone in Wilderness," "Boy Teaches Indian to Read," etc.). Your child may want to include a sports section (e.g., "Hunting with the Indians," "Indian Games," etc.), a comic strip section, illustrations, and weather reports for the area of Maine where Matt lived.

3. Make arrangements to talk with a nutritionist at a hospital or nursing home. Work with your child to prepare several questions about survival to ask the nutritionist. The questions may regard Matt's eating experiences specifically or human health and nutrition in general. As a follow-up activity, work with your child to plan meals for a one-week stay in the wilderness.

Related Children's Books

First Came the Indians by M. J. Wheeler
Linda and the Indians by C. W. Anderson
North America Indians by Marie Gursline

Salt Boy by Mary Perrine
Whale in the Sky by Anne Rose
Zeek Silver Moon by Amy Ehrlich

73

Sky Tree

Thomas Locker
New York: HarperCollins, 1995

Book Summary

This is the story of a tree that stands on a hill by a river. The sky changes, the seasons change, and the tree goes through a series of marvelous transformations. Wonderful paintings highlight significant events during one year in the life of this tree.

Discussion Questions

1. Which illustrations made you feel the happiest, the saddest, the quietest, and the smallest?

2. Why is this tree called the Sky Tree?

3. How is this tree similar to or different from other trees that you have seen?

Activities (Please select one or more activities.)

1. Invite your child to photograph a nearby tree periodically, throughout the year. Ask your child to keep a diary or journal of the changes in the tree. What animals visit or live in the tree? Do the colors of the tree change? What does the tree look like during different weather and seasons? Periodically, discuss with your child any changes in the tree and how those changes may be similar to or different from changes experienced by the Sky Tree.

2. Invite your child to write to the following groups and ask for information on trees:

    Forest Service
    U.S. Department of Agriculture
    P.O. Box 96090
    Washington, DC 20090
    (Ask for the poster "How a Tree Grows")

    National Arbor Day Foundation
    100 Arbor Avenue
    Nebraska City, NE 68410
    (Ask for information on Arbor Day)

3. Invite your child to imagine that he or she is a tree. Ask your child to write a "Life Story" from the perspective of a tree. What happens to a tree during the course of a year? A decade? A century? How is a tree's life similar to or different from a human being's life?

Related Children's Books

The Big Tree by Bruce Hiscock
Crinkleroot's Guide to Knowing the Trees by Jim Arnosky
The Ever-Living Tree by Linda Vieira
A Gift of a Tree by Greg Quinn
Green Giants by Sneed Collard
Outside and Inside Trees by Sandra Markle
Tree by David Burnie
A Tree in a Forest by Jan Thornhill
The Tree in the Ancient Forest by Carol Reed-Jones

The Snowy Day

Ezra Jack Keats
New York: Viking, 1962

Story Summary

This is the story of a day in the life of Peter. He looks out his bedroom window one morning and sees snow everywhere. He spends the day playing in the snow and comes home tired and wet. He is eager to play in the snow again the next day.

Discussion Questions

1. How did Peter feel when he saw the snow outside his window? Would you have felt the same way?

2. Why did Peter decide not to join the big boys in a snowball fight?

3. How would your life be different if it snowed year-round?

4. How did Peter feel when he discovered that his snowball had melted?

5. Do you like snow? Why?

6. How might Peter's day have been different if it had rained instead of snowed?

Activities (Please select one or more activities.)

1. Discuss with your child ways that people keep warm during the winter. Check out books from a public library on winter fashions for various parts of the country or the world. Your child may want to use the book *How to Keep Warm in Winter* by David A. Ross (New York: Crowell, 1980) as a reference.

2. Discuss with your child the role of Peter's mother in the story. How did she feel when Peter was playing in the snow? What was she doing while he was outside? How did she feel when he came inside with wet clothes? How did she feel about the snow? Invite your child to dictate or rewrite the story from the mother's point of view.

3. Ask your child to write a series of "mini-stories" from the snowball's point of view, describing what it feels like to fall from the sky, to be packed into snow, to be stuffed into a pocket, and to melt inside a house. Have your child make a construction paper "pocket" by folding a 9-by-12-inch sheet of paper in half and stapling together the two opposite open sides. Have your child write the stories on large paper "snowballs" and insert them into the pocket when not on display.

4. Have your child write a sequel to *The Snowy Day*, describing Peter's adventures with his friend on the second day of snow. Have your child illustrate the text with paper cut-outs.

Related Children's Books

The First Snowfall by Anne F. Rockwell
It's Snowing It's Snowing by Jack Prelutsky
Katy and the Big Snow by Virginia Lee Burton
Snow Bunny by Bubbi Katz

Snow Company by Marc Harshman
The Snow Parade by Barbara Brenner
A Walk on a Snowy Night by Judy Delton

75

Sounder

William H. Armstrong
New York: Harper & Row, 1969

Story Summary

This is the story of a black sharecropper and his family during the early 1900s in the South. When they face hardship, the sharecropper steals food and is arrested and jailed. Eventually he returns home, but he is crippled. The man dies while on a hunting trip with his faithful dog Sounder. With his master gone, the life goes out of Sounder and he, too, dies a short time later.

Discussion Questions

1. Why was learning to read so important to the boy?

2. How would you feel if you could not read or write?

3. Why did the author not give the boy a name?

4. How would you feel if your favorite pet got shot?

Activities (Please select one or more activities.)

1. The chapters in *Sounder* are untitled. Have your child provide a title for each chapter in the book. Discuss the chapter titles with your child.

2. Your child may want to see the movie version of *Sounder* (available in most large video stores). Discuss with your child similarities or differences between the book and the movie. Was the movie true to the character and intent of the book? Which version was more believable? Which version affected you more emotionally? Would your child rather read the book again or see the movie again?

3. The boy's mother picked walnuts for 15 cents a pound. Purchase a bag of unshelled walnuts from a supermarket. To help your child appreciate the amount of work it took to earn a $1.05 in the story, challenge your child to crack enough walnuts (with a nutcracker) to earn $1.05. Ask your child how he or she would feel about having to earn $10.00 doing this kind of work.

4. Ask your child how he or she would feel about having to walk eight miles to school and eight miles back home? Ask your child how long it would take to walk eight miles. (Take your child to a nearby running track and time a one-mile walk. Multiply the time by eight). Have your child compare that time with his or her normal time for traveling to and from school.

Related Children's Books

The ABC's of Black History by Delores L. Holt
Color Me Brown by Lucille H. Giles
Crossing the Line by William Hooks
Dogs for Working People by Joanna Foster
The Emancipation Proclamation by Earl S. Miers
It Started in Montgomery by Dorothy Sterling
Old Yeller by Fred Gibson

76

Stone Fox

John Reynolds Gardiner
New York: Harper & Row, 1980

Story Summary

This is the story of Willy, who hopes to pay the back taxes on his grandfather's farm with the prize money from a dog sled race.

Discussion Questions

1. If you were Stone Fox, what would you have done when Willy's dog died?

2. How would you have raised the money to pay grandpa's back taxes?

3. If you were Willy, what would you have done when you saw the tax collector in your grandfather's house?

4. What makes Searchlight such a special dog?

Activities (Please select one or more activities.)

1. Have your child think of something special he or she could do for a grandparent or an elder relative or friend. Your child may want to make a coupon book for this person. For example:

   This coupon is worth one hour of help whenever you need me.

   Whenever you need a friend, give me a call.

   This coupon is worth one hug.

2. Ask your child to draw pictures of himself or herself engaged in various activities with a grandparent. Combine these pictures together into a scrapbook and have your child create captions for each illustration. Encourage your child to add illustrations or photographs periodically.

3. You and your child may want to create Native American jewelry: Mix together ¾ cup flour, ½ cup cornstarch, and ½ cup salt. Slowly add warm water until the mixture can be kneaded to reduce stickiness. Roll the mixture into balls to make beads. Pierce each bead with a toothpick or large needle, then allow them to air dry or dry in a slow oven (250 degrees). Paint the beads and string them together into necklaces and bracelets.

Related Children's Books

The Christmas Train by Ivan Gantschev
Grandpa Had a Windmill, Grandma Had a Churn by Louise A. Jackson
Shadow in the Snow by Bill Wallace
Where the Red Fern Grows by Wilson Rawls

77

Surprising Swimmers

Anthony D. Fredericks
Minocqua, WI: NorthWord, 1996

Story Summary

This book provides young scientists with an amazing and fascinating look at some of nature's most unusual creatures. Included are a bird that "flies" underwater, an insect that swims backwards and upside down, snakes that stay underwater for more than three hours, and an animal that spends its entire life on a bubble raft. Colorful illustrations and incredible photographs highlight this engrossing book.

Discussion Questions

1. Which of the 12 animals in this book did you find to be most interesting? What did you learn about that animal?

2. Do any of the animals in this book swim like humans? Would you classify humans as "surprising swimmers"?

3. What other ways (besides walking) do animals travel?

4. What other animals could have been included in this book?

Activities (Please select one or more activities.)

1. Discuss with your child the "Fantastic Facts" included throughout this book. Which facts did your child find to be most amazing? Why? Why did the author include this data?

2. Provide your child with a desk or wall map of the world. Invite your child to write the names of the animals in this book on short pieces of masking tape placed on the countries mentioned in the book. You and your child may want to visit a public or school library and read about other animals that inhabit these countries.

3. There are many phrases and expressions that combine animals and water (e.g., "It's raining cats and dogs," "swims like a fish," "dog paddle"). Invite your child to compile these phrases and expressions into a booklet.

4. Encourage your child to write to the following organizations and request brochures and information on marine conservation:

    The Center for Marine Conservation
    1725 DeSales Street, NW
    Washington, DC 20036

    National Wildlife Federation
    1400 16th Street, NW
    Washington, DC 20036

Related Children's Books

Amazing Fish by Mary Ling
Curious Clownfish by Eric Maddem
Fish by Steve Parker
Killers: Fish by Philip Steele

Life in the Oceans by Herbert Wu
Seashore Life by Christine Lazier
Under the Sea from A to Z by Anne Doubilet
Weird Walkers by Anthony D. Fredericks

Sylvester and the Magic Pebble

William Steig
New York: Windmill, 1969

Story Summary

This is the story of Sylvester Duncan, a young donkey who collects pebbles. One day he gets himself into all kinds of trouble when he discovers a magic pebble. Through a series of fortunate circumstances, Sylvester is eventually reunited with his parents.

Discussion Questions

1. If you had found the magic pebble, what would you have wished for first?

2. What else could Sylvester have done to get away from the lion?

3. How did Sylvester's parents feel when they could not find him?

4. Have you ever felt like Sylvester felt when he couldn't be with his parents? If so, when?

Activities (Please select one or more activities.)

1. Take your child outside to look for pebbles and stones with unusual shapes and colors. Paint some of these stones, if desired. Obtain a large sheet cake box from a local bakery and cut off the top. Paint the inside of the box. When the paint is dry, arrange the stones attractively inside the box. Your child may want to label the stones. Cover the box with plastic wrap to create a display resembling a museum case. Exhibit the stones in a prominent location.

2. The entire family may want to enact this story as a play. Roles to include: Mrs. Duncan, Mr. Duncan, Lion, Sylvester, Neighbors, Police Officers, Children, Wolf, Dog. Props to include: umbrella, picnic basket, ordinary pebbles, magic pebble. Have a neighbor videotape the play.

3. Work with your child to create a family rock garden. Have your child collect a variety of rocks and stones and arrange them attractively in a special place outside. Add a few small plants and flowers and put your child in charge of tending the garden.

Related Children's Books

Doctor De Soto by William Steig
Donkey's Dreadful Day by Irina Hole
The Donkey's Story by Barbara Cohen
The Four Donkeys by Lloyd Alexander
Gorky Rises by William Steig
Spinky Sulks by William Steig
Tiffky Doofky by William Steig

Tales of a Fourth Grade Nothing

Judy Blume
New York: Dutton, 1972

Story Summary

This is the story of nine-year-old Peter, whose life with his two-year-old brother Fudge is often exasperating. Fudge has tantrums, destroys Peter's school work, breaks his own teeth trying to fly, and generally creates mayhem.

Discussion Questions

1. Why is Peter's brother nicknamed Fudge?
2. How would you feel if you lost a pet? Did Peter experience these feelings? Why?
3. If you could spend a day with Peter in New York, what would you do?
4. Is the title *Tales of a Fourth Grade Nothing* appropriate for this story? Why?
5. What would Peter's life be like without Fudge?

Activities (Please select one or more activities.)

1. You and your child may enjoy making some Pretzel Turtles. Be sure your child has plenty of opportunities to work with you in preparing this treat:

Pretzel Turtles

1 package dry yeast	1 egg yolk
$\frac{1}{2}$ teaspoon sugar	2 tablespoons water
$4\frac{1}{2}$ cups flour	coarse salt or sesame seeds
$1\frac{1}{2}$ cups warm water (105–115 degrees)	

Dissolve yeast into $1\frac{1}{2}$ cups warm water. Add sugar and stir until dissolved. Add flour and knead 5–6 minutes. Put the dough in a greased bowl. Cover and let rise until double in size. Divide the dough into 12 pieces and shape into turtles. Blend together the egg yolk and 2 tablespoons water. Brush the pretzels with the mixture and sprinkle on salt or sesame seeds. Place on a cookie sheet and bake at 450 degrees for 12 minutes. Makes 12 pretzels.

2. Have your child look through the classified advertisement section of your local newspaper. Challenge your child to create an original classified advertisement for his or her favorite part of the book, using newspaper advertisements as a guide. For example:

> **FOR SALE cheap:** Little brother, cries without reason. Messes up stuff in bedroom. Good for lots of laughs. $50.00 or best offer. Available immediately. Call Peter at 123-4567 after 4:00 p.m.

(*Tales of a Fourth Grade Nothing* continues on page 82.)

3. Have your child read the book *What Do You Say, Dear? A Book of Manners for All Occasions* by Sesyle Joslin (New York: Scholastic, 1980), a humorous book about manners. Invite your child to create a list of manners that Fudge was lacking. Discuss with your child the importance of manners in everyday life. Is it important for adults to have good manners, too?

Related Children's Books

The Bad Dreams of a Good Girl by Susan Shreve
Blubber by Judy Blume
Deenie by Judy Blume
Don't Touch My Room by Patricia Lakin
Footprints Up My Back by Kristi D. Holl
Forever by Judy Blume
I Wish I Was Sick Too by Franz Brandenberg

80

Tar Beach

Faith Ringgold
New York: Crown, 1991

Story Summary

This is the story of Cassie Lightfoot—she is eight years old and she can fly! She can fly above New York City, and she can fly above a building her father helped build. She can even take her baby brother flying and return to the rooftop—Tar Beach—to awaken upon the quilt on which she has been sleeping. This is a magnificent and marvelous tale about a young girl's dreams and her wishes for her family.

Discussion Questions

1. How does a recent dream you had compare to Cassie's dreams?

2. Do all children have vivid imaginations like Cassie? What do other children dream about?

3. If you could have only one wish come true, what would it be?

4. This book has been honored for its illustrations. How did the illustrations help you enjoy the story more? Which illustration did you most enjoy?

Activities (Please select one or more activities.)

1. You and your child might enjoy making ice cream. Obtain a hand-cranked ice cream freezer and look in any comprehensive cookbook for a recipe. Allow your child to pour the ice cream into the freezer, add the appropriate amounts of ice and salt, and turn the crank until the ice cream is frozen. Conduct a "taste test" comparing this ice cream to ice cream bought in the store.

2. Invite your child to interview someone who lived through the Great Depression (e.g., family member, neighbor, someone from a senior citizen center). Encourage your child to compare life during the Great Depression to life today. What does your child have that children then did not have? What major changes have occurred?

3. Take your child to a store that sells quilts (e.g., department store, antique store). Discuss with your child the different patterns, materials, and designs used in quilt making. Discuss why no two quilts are ever the same.

4. Invite your child to write his or her own "flying" story. What would your child see on the journey? Where would your child want to go? What kind of adventures would your child have?

Related Children's Books

The Keeping Quilt by Patricia Polacco
The Patchwork Quilt by Valerie Flournoy
The Quilt by Ann Jonas
The Quilt Story by Tony Johnston
The Rag Coat by Lauren Mills

The Teacher from the Black Lagoon

Mike Thaler
New York: Scholastic, 1989

Story Summary

It is the first day of school. A young boy wonders who his teacher will be. Imagine his surprise (and that of his classmates) when the teacher turns out to be a fearsome green creature with claws! Horrible things happen to several kids, yet the principal seems unconcerned. A surprise ending adds to the hilarity in this delightful and humorous book.

Discussion Questions

1. How would you feel if you learned that your teacher was "from the Black Lagoon"?
2. Did the ending surprise you? If you had written this story, would you have used the same ending?
3. What was the most terrible thing a teacher ever did to you?
4. What was the young boy's greatest worry?

Activities (Please select one or more activities.)

1. Encourage your child (just for fun) to write a short story titled "The Father/Mother from the Black Lagoon." What events from your child's life could be used as material for a story?
2. Invite your child to discuss the qualifications and qualities of a good teacher. What makes a teacher "outstanding"? What kind of training do teachers require? What do teachers need to know about children and how they learn?
3. Before your child reads the book, reveal only the title of the book. Invite your child to prepare an illustration of his or her "Teacher from the Black Lagoon." How does your child's illustration compare with those in the book? Is your child's illustration similar to anyone he or she knows?
4. Invite your child to prepare an advertisement or commercial promoting the book to his or her friends. What type of information should be included to "sell" the book to others? Should the advertisement/commercial be humorous or serious?

Related Children's Books

"Could Be Worse" by James Stevenson
The Gym Teacher from the Black Lagoon by Mike Thaler
Miss Nelson Is Back by Harry Allard
Miss Nelson Is Missing by Harry Allard
Prince Cinders by Babette Cole
Princess Smartypants by Babette Cole
The Principal from the Black Lagoon by Mike Thaler

82

The Three Bears

Paul Galdone
New York: Seabury, 1972

Story Summary

This is the traditional story of Goldilocks and the three bears. Paul Galdone details the adventures (or misadventures) of Goldilocks as she breaks into the house of the three bears. Delightful illustrations highlight this retelling.

Discussion Questions

1. If you were the little "wee bear," how would you have felt about Goldilocks eating all of your porridge, breaking your chair, and messing up your bed?

2. What would the bears have done to Goldilocks if she had not run away?

3. Do you think the three bears will leave their door unlocked again? Why?

4. What would you have done if you had found a stranger sleeping in your bed?

5. Would you want to have Goldilocks as a friend? Why?

Activities (Please select one or more activities.)

1. Invite your child to create a sequel to this story titled *Goldilocks Returns*. What adventures would Goldilocks have during her return visit?

2. Have your child imagine that there are three Goldilockses and one bear. How would the story be different? Ask your child to dictate or write a new version of the tale.

3. Work with your child to make a simple identification card (similar to a driver's license) that could be used in case he or she ever got lost. You may want to take your child to a police station and talk with an officer about what to do if one gets lost.

4. Invite family members to enact a play version of *The Three Bears* using simple props (e.g., chairs, beds, bowls, etc.) and simple actions. Videotape the play and show it to friends and neighbors.

5. Take your child to a grocery store and count the number of times the word *bear* appears in names of food products (e.g., bear cereals, bear cookies). Have your child make a list of these products.

Related Children's Books by Paul Galdone

Henny Penny
The Horse, the Fox, and the Lion
The Little Red Hen
The Monkey and the Crocodile
Three Aesop Fox Fables
The Three Billy Goats Gruff
The Three Little Pigs

Thunder Cake

Patricia Polacco
New York: Philomel, 1990

Story Summary

This is the story of a little girl who is afraid of an approaching storm. With the help of her grandmother, she learns how to determine the distance of the storm and how to bake a "Thunder Cake," which must be in the oven before the storm arrives. This is a marvelous story about overcoming fears and about the special bond that exists between generations.

Discussion Questions

1. What scares you? Why?

2. How do you overcome your fears?

3. Do either of the two characters in this book remind you of anyone you know?

4. Was the grandmother "fooling" her granddaughter?

5. What will the girl do the next time a storm arrives?

Activities (Please select one or more activities.)

1. Invite your child to create sound effects for thunder and rain (e.g., your child may want to beat on a cookie sheet to simulate the sound of thunder, or tap on the plastic lid of a coffee can to simulate the sound of rain). Record an audio version of the story: Read the story again and have your child contribute sound effects.

2. The book contains a recipe for "Thunder Cake." Prepare the cake with your child. Serve the cake to the family and invite your child to retell the story.

3. You and your child may enjoy sharing other books by Patricia Polacco, including *Just Plain Fancy*, *Mrs. Katz and Tush*, *Babushka's Doll*, *Pink and Say*, and *Rechenka's Eggs*. Discuss the distinctive illustrative style of these books.

4. The next time a storm comes through your area, invite your child to count the seconds between a flash of lightning and the clap of thunder. Invite your child to use this measure of time to calculate the distance of an approaching storm as the girl did in the story.

Related Children's Books

Brave Irene by William Steig
The Ghost-Eye Tree by Bill Martin Jr. and John Archambault
Grandma Gets Grumpy by Anna Hines
The Storm Book by Charlotte Zolotow
Storm in the Night by Mary Stolz

Tikki Tikki Tembo

Arlene Mosel
New York: Scholastic, 1968

Story Summary

This is the story of a Chinese family who believe that a long name is better than a short name. An almost tragic incident convinces them otherwise.

Discussion Questions

1. How would the story be different if Tikki Tikki Tembo had fallen into the ocean?
2. Can you think of some other titles for this book?
3. What did you like most about this story? Would you want to read it again?

Activities (Please select one or more activities.)

1. Visit a public library or bookstore with your child and obtain a name book. Help your child find the names of family members, relatives, and friends. Explain the meaning of each person's name. You and your child may want to create a "Family Name Dictionary" outlining the meaning of each family member's name.

2. Discuss with your child how your family's lifestyle compares to Tikki Tikki Tembo's lifestyle. What are the similarities and differences?

3. Ask your child to pretend that you and he or she are newspaper reporters assigned to cover Tikki Tikki Tembo's "well incident." Show your child sample newspaper headlines from your local paper and ask your child to invent a headline for this incident. Work with your child to write an imaginary newspaper story.

Related Children's Books

Brothers by Florence B. Freedman
The Enchanted Tapestry by Robert D. San Succi
Even That Moose Won't Listen to Me by Martha G. Alexander
Jimmy Lee Did It! by Pat Cummings
Little Brother, No More by Robert Benton
The Mommy Exchange by Colin Hawkins
My Brother, Will by Joan Robins
A Place for Ben by Jeanne Titherington
The Terrible Thing That Happened at Our House by Marge Blaine
The Trouble with Mom by Babette Cole

The True Confessions of Charlotte Doyle

Avi

New York: Orchard, 1990

Story Summary

This is the story of Charlotte Doyle, a 13-year-old girl who sets sail from England in 1832 to join her family in America. Through her journal, the reader learns about life on the sea and a revolt against the ship's captain— and the ensuing consequences. Told in the first person, this book is filled with suspense and excitement. A controversial ending highlights this well-crafted story.

Discussion Questions

1. What impressed you most about Charlotte? What part of her personality most resembles your personality?

2. What difficulties did people endure on long ocean voyages in the 1800s?

3. Would you have wanted to be a passenger on that ship? Would you have wanted to be a member of the crew?

4. How did your impression of Charlotte change from the beginning of the story to the end?

Activities (Please select one or more activities.)

1. Encourage your child to keep a journal or diary over a predetermined length of time (one month, several months, one year). What events in your child's life would he or she want to write about? Discuss with your child reasons why people keep journals or diaries. What do journals and diaries reveal about the person writing them?

2. Invite your child to visit a public or school library and check out books on sailing ships of the nineteenth century. Encourage your child to look for illustrations of these ships. What are the similarities and differences among ships of the nineteenth century? How do these ships compare to the illustration of the *Seahawk* at the back of *The True Confessions of Charlotte Doyle*?

3. Your child may enjoy building a model of a sailing ship (available at craft and hobby stores). Work with your child to construct the model while discussing ideas about the real-life construction process and functions of various parts of the ship.

4. Discuss with your child how life for young girls in the nineteenth century was different from life for girls today. How have girls' lives changed? Is life for girls better today?

Related Children's Books

The Dark Canoe by Scott O'Dell
The Island by Gary Paulsen
Nothing but the Truth by Avi
The Private Worlds of Julia Redfern
   by Eleanor Cameron

Sarah Bishop by Scott O'Dell
Seafaring Women by Linda Grant DePauw
The Voyage of the Frog by Gary Paulsen
The Witch of Blackbird Pond
   by Elizabeth George Speare

86

The True Story of the 3 Little Pigs by A. Wolf

Jon Scieszka
New York: Penguin, 1989

Story Summary

This is a riotous retelling of the classic tale about the big bad wolf and the three little pigs—but this time the wolf gets to tell his side of the story. The wolf acts as his own reporter, to ensure that the facts are correct. The result is an uproariously funny story that children will want to read again and again.

Discussion Questions

1. What was the funniest part of this story? Explain.
2. How does this story differ from the original version of *The Three Little Pigs*?
3. If you were to write a letter to Jon Scieszka, what would you write?
4. If you could give the story a different ending, what would it be?

Activities (Please select one or more activities.)

1. Invite your child to select a familiar story (e.g., *The Three Billy Goats Gruff*, *Little Red Riding Hood*, *Cinderella*, *Hansel and Gretel*). Encourage your child to retell or rewrite a version of the selected story from the point of view of a character other than the narrator (e.g., *Cinderella* might be told from the point of view of one of the three stepsisters, *Little Red Riding Hood* might be told from the grandmother's point of view, *Jack and the Beanstalk* might be told from the giant's point of view). Have your child share the retelling with the family.

2. Invite your child to select a familiar nursery rhyme or fairy tale and rewrite it as a newspaper article. How would a newspaper reporter write a story about a little girl (in a red riding hood) traveling through the forest on her way to her grandmother's house? How would a reporter handle a story about a woman named Snow White who works for seven tiny men?

3. This story begins when the wolf runs out of sugar while baking a cake for his granny's birthday. Work with your child to prepare a birthday cake for the wolf's granny. Have a special celebration and sing "Happy Birthday" in honor of the grandmother wolf.

Related Children's Books

Frantic Frogs and Other Frankly Fractured Folktales for Reader's Theatre by Anthony D. Fredericks
The Frog Prince Continued by Jon Scieszka
The Paper Bag Princess by Robert Munsch
The Stinky Cheese Man and Other Fairly Stupid Tales by Jon Scieszka
The Teacher from the Black Lagoon by Mike Thaler

Tuesday

David Wiesner
New York: Clarion, 1991

Story Summary

This is a story about frogs. One Tuesday evening, while the frogs are peacefully sleeping on the pond, they suddenly find themselves aloft on flying lily pads. They navigate through open windows and past large dogs. Then, just as suddenly as it began, their magical flight is over, and they must hop home. A sparse text and humorous illustrations highlight this imaginative, award-winning book.

Discussion Questions

1. Why do you think the author relied so heavily on illustrations, and so little on words, to tell this story?

2. Is it possible to tell an entire story with pictures?

3. What will happen on the following Tuesday?

4. If you could take a magical flight, where would you go?

Activities (Please select one or more activities.)

1. Invite your child to retell this story by creating several sentences for each page of the book. Discuss with your child any difficulties he or she may experience. Do the illustrations alone provide enough "information" for the reader?

2. Invite your child to keep a diary or journal of events that occur on several Tuesdays (e.g., three consecutive Tuesdays). Encourage your child to review these events and select one as the basis for a written or oral magical adventure to share with the family.

3. Invite your child to make a list of all the emotions expressed in this book. Why did the author/illustrator express these emotions on the faces of the characters rather than in words? If your child were portrayed as a character in this book, what emotions would he or she express? How would these emotions be illustrated?

Related Children's Books

Free Fall by David Wiesner
Half a Moon and One Whole Star by Crescent Dragonwagon
Night in the Country by Cynthia Rylant
Nora's Stars by Satomi Ichikawa
Rainy Day Dream by Michael Chesworth
Tar Beach by Faith Ringgold
The Trek by Ann Jonas

88

The Ugly Duckling

Hans Christian Andersen
New York: Harcourt Brace Jovanovich, 1979

Story Summary

This is the time-honored story of a swan who is misplaced into a nest of ducklings. Because he looks different than the other ducklings, he is taunted and teased. He eventually leaves the nest to find his own kind.

Discussion Questions

1. Is it more important to be beautiful on the inside or on the outside?

2. Was the swan treated fairly?

3. How would you feel if nobody liked you?

4. How did the ending of the story make you feel?

5. What might have happened if the swan had not been able to find his relatives?

Activities (Please select one or more activities.)

1. Work with your child to make paper bag puppets of swans. Re-create a portion of the story using the puppets. Invite your child to create original dialogue.

2. Invite your child to create a model of a castle using cardboard boxes, paints, pebbles, toothpicks, and other art materials. Invite family members to help.

3. Discuss with your child how he or she felt after reading this story. Is there anything in the story that might apply to your child? What does your child have in common with the Ugly Duckling? Has your child experienced anything similar to the adventures of the Ugly Duckling?

4. Photograph your child over a period of several days. Mount each photograph on a separate piece of paper and ask your child to supply captions or titles. Discuss the similarities and differences among the photographs. Is it possible to look better one day in comparison to other days?

Related Children's Books

Gray Duck Catches a Friend by Vicki Artis
Leo the Late Bloomer by Robert Kraus
Make Way for Ducklings by Robert McCloskey
A Story About Ping by Marjorie Flack
Who Will Be My Friend? by Syd Hoff

The Velveteen Rabbit

Margery Williams
New York: Doubleday, 1971

Story Summary

This is a delightful story about a boy's love for his stuffed velveteen rabbit. He claims that his bunny is real—something all playthings long to be. By the end of the story, not only is the rabbit real to the boy, but he is also real to everyone.

Discussion Questions

1. Were you satisfied with the ending? What would you change?
2. If you could have any stuffed toy come to life, which toy would it be?
3. Would you want to have a velveteen rabbit?
4. How did the velveteen rabbit become real to the boy?

Activities (Please select one or more activities.)

1. Encourage your child to write a short story about one of his or her toys suddenly becoming real. Which toy would your child choose? What adventures would your child and the toy have?
2. Ask your child to prepare a classified advertisement for a missing stuffed toy. Show your child advertisements in a newspaper as examples and encourage your child to create an original advertisement.
3. Visit a public library with your child and conduct research on rabbits. Your child might want to create a "Rabbit Book": Have your child fill the book with pictures, facts, and related information, fictional and nonfictional, about rabbits (e.g., favorite rabbit book titles, foods rabbits eat, names of famous rabbits, where rabbits live, different varieties of rabbits, rabbit habitats, etc.). For added effect, have your child cut out two similar cardboard rabbit shapes and use them for the covers of the book.

Related Children's Books

The Christmas Bunny by William Lipkind
Sleepy Time Bunny by Stephen Cosgrove
Snowy the Rabbit by Stephen Hynard
The Snuggle Bunny by Nancy Jewell
Too Many Rabbits by Peggy Parish
The World of Rabbits by Jennifer Coldrey

90

The Very Hungry Caterpillar

Eric Carle
New York: Crowell, 1976

Story Summary

This is the story of a caterpillar. It is born on a leaf and eats various foods until it is so full that it builds a cocoon. The caterpillar finally hatches as a beautiful butterfly. This book introduces the concepts of the life cycle of a butterfly, the days of the week, and nutrition in a simple way.

Discussion Questions

1. What part of the story did you most enjoy?

2. Would you want to learn more about caterpillars? What in particular?

3. What are your favorite foods?

4. If you could change into something else, what would it be?

Activities (Please select one or more activities.)

1. Your child might enjoy making a caterpillar. Provide your child with jelly beans, tiny plastic eyes, small pieces of pipe cleaners, glue, and a toothpick. Have your child make the body of a caterpillar by sticking jelly beans onto a toothpick. Stick in pipe cleaners (antennae) and glue on eyes.

2. Find a baby picture of your child. Glue the picture onto a large sheet of paper and have your child draw a caterpillar using the picture as its head. Color the caterpillar with crayons or watercolor paint and display the picture.

3. Drape a sheet over a clothesline or between two chairs. Crawl inside with your child and retell the story. Discuss how it might feel to be inside a cocoon for an extended period of time.

4. Take your child for a walk around the house to look for caterpillars. They can usually be found on trees in warm weather. Have your child observe and record how caterpillars act in their natural environment and then collect them in jars for further observation. Your child may want to decorate the jars with fabric, paint, pens, and ribbon.

5. Have your child write a sequel to *The Very Hungry Caterpillar* about the caterpillar's life as a butterfly.

Related Children's Books

Caterpillars by Dorothy Sterling
Caterpillars and How They Live by Robert M. McClung
A First Look at Caterpillars by Millicent Ellis Selsam
I Like Caterpillars by Gladys Conklin
The Pet in the Jar by Judy Stang

91

The Village of Round and Square Houses
Ann Grifalconi
Boston: Little, Brown, 1986

Story Summary
In the Cameroons of Central Africa exists an isolated village named Tos. In this village the women live in round houses and the men live in square houses. The story of how this came to be is told through the eyes of a young girl.

Discussion Questions
1. How is the village of Tos similar to the town or city where you live?

2. How is the narrator similar to you, a family member, or one of your friends?

3. How do such natural events as erupting volcanoes and earthquakes change the way people live?

Activities (Please select one or more activities.)
1. You and your child may want to create a chemical volcano. Outdoors, place a small coffee cup into sand or dirt. Pour 1 tablespoon of liquid detergent into the cup. Add a few drops of red food coloring, 1 cup of vinegar, and enough warm water to fill the cup almost to the top. Quickly add 2 tablespoons of baking soda to the cup to make the volcano "erupt."

2. Invite your child to look through a newspaper for articles and information relating to eruptions of volcanoes. Invite your child to cut out this information and assemble it into an ongoing journal. Have your child share the journal with others periodically.

3. Obtain a copy of *Volcanoes* by Seymour Simon (New York: Mulberry, 1988) from a school or public library. Read this book with your child and discuss the forces that create a volcano and how these forces may have created the volcano in *The Village of Round and Square Houses*.

Related Children's Books
Earthquakes and Volcanoes by Fiona Watt
Mountains and Volcanoes by Barbara Taylor
Surtsey: The Newest Place on Earth by Kathryn Lasky
Volcano: The Eruption and Healing of Mount St. Helens by Patricia Lauber

92

The Wall

Eve Bunting
New York: Clarion, 1990

Story Summary

This is the story of a boy and his father who visit the Vietnam Veterans Memorial in Washington, DC. While they search for the grandfather's name on the wall they meet a man without legs and a sad old couple. Finally, they locate the name they have been searching for and make a rubbing. This is a touching story about the victims of war as told through the eyes of a young boy. This book will have an emotional effect on children and adults alike.

Discussion Questions

1. How did the boy change from the beginning of the story to the end?
2. What did the boy learn from the other characters in the story?
3. Why was this memorial erected? What can people learn from the Vietnam Veterans Memorial?
4. If you could write or say something to the boy in the story, what would you share?

Activities (Please select one or more activities.)

1. Discuss with your child the emotions he or she felt while listening to the story. What emotions did you, the parent, experience while sharing the story? How are your emotions similar to your child's feelings?
2. Visit a public or school library and introduce your child to other books by Eve Bunting, including *Fly Away Home* and *How Many Days to America? A Thanksgiving Story*. Discuss similar themes in the stories that Eve Bunting writes.
3. Often, the lasting effect of this book occurs after several readings. You and your child may want to read the book repeatedly over a period of several days. Discuss with your child his or her feelings and how they change over the course of several readings.
4. Encourage your child to interview a veteran of the Vietnam War (contact the local chapter of the Veterans of Foreign Wars—the V.F.W.—in your town or local area). What does the veteran remember about the war? How did the war affect him or her? What does he or she think about the Vietnam Veterans Memorial?

Related Children's Books

Fallen Angels by Walter Dean Myers
The Great Peace March by Holly Near
Hiroshima No Pika by Junko Morimoto
Park's Quest by Katherine Paterson
Peace Begins with You by Katherine Scholes
Sadako and the Thousand Paper Cranes by Eleanor Coerr
The Story of the Vietnam Memorial by David Wright

The Wednesday Surprise

Eve Bunting
New York: Clarion, 1989

Story Summary

This is the story of Anna, whose Wednesday nights are special: Grandma comes over with a big, lumpy bag filled with books. Together they read story after story, all the while planning a surprise for Dad's birthday.

Discussion Questions

1. Why did Anna's grandmother want to learn to read?
2. Why was Anna's father so happy?
3. If Anna's grandmother could relive her life, what would she do differently?
4. What are your favorite family memories?
5. What are your favorite birthday memories?

Activities (Please select one or more activities.)

1. Invite your child to create a scrapbook of activities he or she enjoys doing with grandparents. The scrapbook might include photographs with accompanying captions as well as illustrations of holidays or family gatherings.

2. Encourage your child to create an oath in which he or she agrees to read with you for at least 15 minutes each day. Your child may want to write a contract to support the oath.

3. Your child might enjoy creating a family newspaper. Assign your child the role of reporter and ask him or her to interview family members about their opinions of current issues, selected hobbies, free-time activities, vacation spots, and so on. Assemble the information on each family member into a sheet of news and assemble all the sheets into a family newspaper.

4. Encourage your child to create a collage of all the important things that are necessary to make a family (e.g., love, sharing, conversation, listening, caring, etc.). Have your child cut out pictures and words from old magazines and glue them to a sheet of posterboard.

Related Children's Books

Behave Yourself, Bethany Brant by Patricia Beatty
A Gift for Mama by Esther Hautzig
Grandma and Grandpa by Helen Oxenbury
One Sister Too Many by Carol Adler
The Two of Them by Aliki

94

Weird Walkers

Anthony D. Fredericks
Minocqua, WI: NorthWord, 1996

Story Summary

This book presents some of the most unusual animals on earth. Readers meet a fish that walks out of the water, a lizard that walks on the water, and a tree that "walks" through the water. Information on protecting the environments of these special creatures is also included.

Discussion Questions

1. Which of the 12 animals in this book did you find to be most unusual?

2. Do you know of other "weird walkers" that should be included in a book of this type?

3. What are some unusual means of transportation that other animals use?

Activities (Please select one or more activities.)

1. Invite your child to write to the following environmental agencies to obtain relevant literature on endangered species around the world. When the material arrives, invite your child to make a list of the animals that are most seriously imperiled, those that are endangered, and those that are threatened.

   National Wildlife Federation
   8925 Leesburg Pike
   Vienna, VA 22184

   National Audubon Society
   666 Pennsylvania Avenue, SE
   Washington, DC 20003

2. Invite your child to make a large chart on an oversized piece of posterboard that lists the speeds at which selected animals travel. The chart might rank animals from the fastest to the slowest or vice versa.

3. Invite your child to measure the different speeds (walk, trot, run) at which a family pet travels. Have your child use a stopwatch to time the family pet over a measured course and determine its speed in miles per hour. Have your child make a chart or graph of the different speeds.

Related Children's Books

Amazing Butterflies and Moths by John Still
Amazing Crocodiles and Reptiles by Mary Ling
Animal Tracks by Arthur Dorros
Can Birds Get Lost? and Other Questions About Animals by Jack Myers
Creepy Crawlies by Ruth Thompson

Welcome to the Green House

Jane Yolen
New York: Putnam, 1993

Story Summary

Through the use of poetic language the reader is introduced to the wonders, beauty, and majesty of the world's rain forests. The inhabitants of this fragile ecosystem and the colors, sights, and sounds of day-to-day life are all magically revealed in this wonderful tribute to a magnificent environment.

Discussion Questions

1. What was the most amazing thing you learned about the rain forest?

2. Do you like the illustrations in this book? Do they captured the romance of the rain forest?

3. How does this book differ from other books you have read about the rain forest?

4. Would you want to visit a rain forest? Explain.

Activities (Please select one or more activities.)

1. Invite your child to take a walk around the house or through the community and make a list of all the animals he or she sees. When your child returns, invite him or her to make a list of all the animals mentioned in this book. Which list is longer? Do any animals appear on both lists? Are there animals in the book that your child has never seen or heard of before?

2. The rain forest is filled with butterflies. You and your child may enjoy raising your own butterflies. The following kits are available from Delta Education (P.O. Box 3000, Nashua, NH 03061-3000; 1-800-442-5444): Butterfly Tower (catalog # 53-021-2288) and Butterfly Garden (catalog # 53-020-6007). You and your child may also want to order a Butterfly Feeder from Delta Education (catalog # 53-060-3877) to attract butterflies to your house.

3. Invite your child to write to the following groups to request information and brochures on rain forest preservation:

Children's Rainforest
P.O. Box 936
Lewiston, ME 04240

Rainforest Action Network
450 Sansome Street
San Francisco, CA 94111

Save the Rainforest
604 Jamie Street
Dodgeville, WI 53533

Welcome to the Green House— Continued

4. Many foods are obtained from the rain forest. Provide your child with the following list and invite him or her to look for these foods in your kitchen or in a grocery store: bananas, pineapples, papayas, sugar, guavas, mangoes, coconuts, chicle (chewing gum), cinnamon, cantaloupes, oranges, and tomatoes.

Related Children's Books

At Home in the Rain Forest by Madeline Dunphy
Exploring the Rainforest by Anthony D. Fredericks
The Great Kapok Tree by Lynne Cherry
One Day in the Tropical Rain Forest by Jean Craighead George
The Rain Forest Book by Scott Lewis
Tropical Rain Forests Around the World by Elaine Landau
Why Are the Rain Forests Vanishing? by Isaac Asimov
Why Save the Rain Forest? by Donald M. Silver

From *The Librarian's Complete Guide to Involving Parents Through Children's Literature.* © 1997. Libraries Unlimited. (800) 237-6124.

When I Was Young in the Mountains

Cynthia Rylant
New York: Dutton, 1982

Story Summary

This is the story of a young girl growing up in Appalachia. The story details the lives of mountain people, the relationships of friends and family, and the effect rural living has on the girl.

Discussion Questions

1. Would you enjoy living in the mountains?

2. How would your daily life be different if you had no running water or indoor plumbing?

3. What do you do every day that you would not be able to do if you lived where the girl did?

4. How is the store in this story different from the store in your town or neighborhood?

Activities (Please select one or more activities.)

1. Take your child on a "nature walk" through a park or the school grounds. Invite your child to collect various objects along the way, such as rocks, leaves, and flowers. Visit a public library with your child to obtain books on plant and animal life in your area of the country. How do the plants and animals in your part of the country compare to those mentioned in the story?

2. Your child may enjoy making leaf rubbings. Provide your child with a piece of newsprint or tracing paper. Place the paper over a leaf and rub over the paper with a crayon until the full impression of the leaf is shown. Have your child label each rubbing with the name and a description of the tree or plant that bears the leaf. Collect these rubbings into a scrapbook and have your child add rubbings throughout the year.

3. Your child may want to start a rock collection. Have your child begin by collecting rocks in your neighborhood. Starter kits of various rocks can be obtained from Edmund Scientific (101 East Gloucester Pike, Barrington, NJ 08007) and Hubbard Scientific Company (P.O. Box 104, Northbrook, IL 60065).

Related Children's Books

The Girl by Robbie Branscum
Hills and Mountains by Mark Steep
The Mountain Bluebird by Ron Hirschi
The Mountain of Adventure by Enid Blyton
The People Therein by Mildred Lee
Poems of the Old West: A Rocky Mountain Anthology by Levette Jay Davidson

Where the Sidewalk Ends

Shel Silverstein
New York: Harper & Row, 1974

Story Summary

Get set for lots of laughs, tons of giggles, and loads of smiles. This collection of poetry concerns all the things that matter to kids— bratty little sisters, not wanting to go to school, making a mess at the dinner table, and incredibly lovable monsters. This book is a guaranteed winner with kids of all ages.

Discussion Questions

1. Which poem most reminded you of yourself? For which poem could *you* have been the narrator?

2. If you had an opportunity to say anything to Shel Silverstein, what would you say?

3. Is there a specific poem your friends would enjoy? Why?

Activities (Please select one or more activities.)

1. Share the poem "Sick" with your child. Invite your child to create other "diseases" or "ailments" that might have been included in this poem. Discuss why this particular poem is a favorite of many children.

2. Discuss with your child some of the strange and unusual characters in this book. Which character is most unusual? Which character is most like a member of the family? Which family member would your child want to write a poem about?

3. Invite your child to write an original poem using one of the poems in this book as a model. For example, your child may want to use "Boa Constrictor" as a model for a poem that begins: "Oh, I'm being eaten by the family dog." The poem "Recipe for a Hippopotamus Sandwich" can be used as a model for a poem that begins: "A *hamster* sandwich is easy to make."

4. Make poetry reading a regular part of your sharing time. Share at least one poem each week with your child. *Where the Sidewalk Ends*, as well as the titles listed below, will open your child's eyes (and ears) to the magic of poetry for a lifetime.

Related Children's Books

Beastly Boys and Ghastly Girls by William Cole
Did Adam Name the Vinegarroon? by X. J. Kennedy
Falling Up by Shel Silverstein
If I Were in Charge of the World and Other Worries by Judith Viorst
A Light in the Attic by Shel Silverstein
The New Kid on the Block by Jack Prelutsky

Where the Wild Things Are

Maurice Sendak
New York: Harper Row, 1963

Story Summary

This is the story of a night in the life of a small boy named Max. Sent to his bed without his supper, Max imagines himself to be the master of the wild things. The smell of his dinner being brought to his room brings him back from monsterland.

Discussion Questions

1. What could Max have done to be sent to bed without supper?

2. Would you want to visit the land of the wild things? Why?

3. Why did Max become king of all the wild things?

4. Will Max ever go back to visit the wild things?

5. Would your friends enjoy this book? Why?

Activities (Please select one or more activities.)

1. Have your child pretend to be a reporter who has just spotted the wild things for the first time. Direct your child to write a newspaper-style article that includes who, what, and where in the first sentence (e.g., "A mysterious, 10-foot-tall creature called a 'wild thing' was spotted yesterday by a group of vacationing reporters in the jungle of Forty Winks.").

2. Work with your child to create a "scary costume" catalog. Ask your child to draw several examples of scary costumes. Look through old magazines for pictures of outfits that could be used as part of a scary costume. Put together a catalog that offers a variety of costumes for those in the Land of the Wild Things.

3. Have your child brainstorm all the places that a monster or nightmare could hide in his or her room. Ask your child to draw up a plan for "monster proofing" the bedroom. Compile all ideas into a "how-to" manual for children who worry about monsters at night.

4. Your child may enjoy reading other books by Maurice Sendak, including *In the Night Kitchen*, *Chicken Soup with Rice*, and *Rosie and Michael*.

Related Children's Books

Daddy Is a Monster . . . Sometimes by John Steptoe
The Dream Child by David McPhail
A Monster in the Mailbox by Sheila Gordon
My Mama Says There Aren't Any Zombies, Ghosts, Vampires, Creatures, Demons, Monsters, Fiends, Goblins, or Things by Judith Viorst
The Night Flight by Joanne Ryder
Spence and the Sleeptime Monster by Christa Chevalier

99

The Whipping Boy
Sid Fleischman
New York: Greenwillow, 1986

Story Summary

Jemmy, who must be whipped every time the prince gets into trouble, leads the young highness through the forests and sewers of old England in this adventure filled with suspense, strange characters, and the coming of age of "Prince Brat."

Discussion Questions

1. What would you enjoy most about living during the time period of this story? Why?

2. Is "Prince Brat" similar to anyone you know? Explain.

3. What adventures might the two boys have in a sequel to this story?

4. How would Prince Brat's inability to read have been a problem for him later in his life?

Activities (Please select one or more activities.)

1. Invite your child to create an imaginary journal that could have been written by the prince (if he could write). Entries might include his adventures with Jemmy, the characters they saw along the way, and how they eventually settled their differences.

2. Encourage your child to check a phone book and make a list of the modern-day services that might be used by royalty. The list might include carpet cleaning services (for the red carpet), catering services, transportation services, and so on.

3. Invite your child to pretend to be a reporter covering the "kidnapping" of the prince. What facts or details should be included in a television broadcast? What facts would be appropriate for a newspaper article?

4. Invite your child to investigate differences between sanitation and waste disposal during the time period of this story and sanitation and waste disposal today. Has the nature of waste products changed? Why is sanitation such an important environmental issue?

5. Encourage your child to construct an imaginary map of the prince's kingdom. Have your child include all the sites mentioned in the story as well as any others that would be important in a kingdom.

Related Children's Books

Alan Garner's Book of British Fairy Tales by Alan Garner
A Bag of Moonshine by Alan Garner
British Folktales by Katherine Briggs
British Folk Tales by Kevin Crossley-Holland

Why Mosquitoes Buzz in People's Ears

Verna Aardema
New York: Dial, 1975

Story Summary

This 1976 Caldecott Medal winner is a West African tale about a mosquito who sets off a chain of events in the jungle that leads to disaster. As a result, the mosquito is destined to buzz in people's ears forever.

Discussion Questions

1. How would you describe the mosquito's personality?

2. If you could be any animal in the story, which one would you be?

3. What kind of advice would you want to give the mosquito?

4. Would you recommend this book to your friends? Why?

5. How would the story be different if it had taken place in a zoo?

Activities (Please select one or more activities.)

1. Your child may want to create a handbook on Africa. Have your child cut the cover of the book (from a large sheet of cardboard) into the shape of Africa. Visit a public library to obtain information about Africa (e.g., agriculture, city life, land regions—deserts, forests, grasslands, transportation, family life, etc.). Have your child print or type the information on separate sheets of paper for each topic. Bind together the pages and the cover to make a book.

2. Encourage your child to create an original written or oral folktale to explain phenomena in our everyday lives (e.g., "Why flies always land on our food," "Why the birds always chirp," "Why wild animals always run from humans," or "Why cats always sleep during the day"). Your child may want to share the story with the family.

3. Your child may enjoy singing popular African songs in an African language. Check with a public librarian to obtain a copy of *Call and Response Rhythmic Group Singing* (New York: Folkways Records, 1957), a recording by Ella Jenkins. This record is designed so that children repeat the words in rhythm and thus experience the language and music of Africa firsthand.

4. You and your child may want to have an African foods celebration for the entire family. Purchase a variety of foods native to Africa: honey, dates, coffee, cloves (also try clove gum), yams, sunflower seeds, peanuts, grapes, and olives. Have your child arrange the foods attractively and encourage the family to try everything.

Related Children's Books

Animals in the Jungle by Kenneth Lilly
In the Jungle by Eugene Booth
Jungles by Clive Catchpole
Jungles by John Norris Wood

101

A Wrinkle in Time

Madeleine L'Engle
New York: Farrar, Straus & Giroux, 1962

Story Summary

Meg and Charles search for their father with the aid of a tesseract. Along the way they do battle with an evil darkness that threatens the cosmos.

Discussion Questions

1. If you could tesser, where would you tesser to?

2. Would you want to live on Camazotz?

3. How would you react if you came across It?

4. Why did the author include the twins (Sandy and Denny) in the story?

5. What do think about Charles Wallace's gift? Would you want to have it? Why?

Activities (Please select one or more activities.)

1. Ask your child to select several different scenes from the story to develop into an oversize mural. Provide your child with a large sheet of newsprint (available at newspaper offices or hobby stores) and art materials.

   Example scenes:

   > The planet of Camazotz
   >
   > The two-dimensional planet
   >
   > Aunt Beast
   >
   > It
   >
   > The planet of Uriel
   >
   > The reunion of the Murry's
   >
   > Mrs. Who
   >
   > Mrs. Whatsit
   >
   > Mrs. Which
   >
   > The Black Thing
   >
   > The man with Red Eyes

(*A Wrinkle in Time* continues on page 106.)

2. Work with your child to create a story map about the book. A story map is a series of sentence "stems" that can be completed with terms, words, or phrases from the story or from the reader's own interpretation of the story. For example:

The story began with _____.

The major character did _____.

The conflict was _____.

The conflict was resolved _____.

Other characters in the story were _____.

They did _____ in the story.

3. Mrs. Whatsit is 2,379,152,497 years old. Discuss with your child the average life span of a human being. Encourage your child to discuss what he or she hopes to accomplish during his or her lifetime.

Related Children's Books

The Arm of the Starfish by Madeleine L'Engle
The Farthest Shore Ursula LeGuin
A Swiftly Tilting Planet by Madeleine L'Engle
A Wind in the Door by Madeleine L'Engle
The Witch of Blackbird Pond by Elizabeth George Speare

Appendix

Supplemental Booklists for Parents

Grades Preschool–Kindergarten

Dear Parents:

Following is a list of 95 books highly recommended for children in preschool and kindergarten. These books have been selected on the basis of their appropriateness to children's interests and represent a wide range of award-winning and frequently cited books for this age level. Plan to visit the public library or your child's school library regularly and make these suggestions part of your child's reading adventures and explorations.

Ackerman, Karen. *Song and Dance Man*. New York: Knopf, 1988.

Ahlberg, Janet, and Allan Ahlberg. *Each Peach Pear Plum*. New York: Penguin, 1978.

Aliki. *We Are Best Friends*. New York: Greenwillow, 1982.

Bang, Molly. *Ten, Nine, Eight*. New York: Greenwillow, 1983.

Barrett, Judi. *Animals Should Definitely Not Wear Clothing*. New York: Atheneum, 1970.

Bauley, Lorinda Bryan. *Jack and the Beanstalk*. New York: Putnam, 1983.

Bennett, David. *One Cow Moo Moo*. New York: Holt, 1990.

Borden, Louise. *Caps, Hats, Socks, and Mittens*. New York: Scholastic, 1989.

Brown, Marc. *Arthur's Baby*. New York: Joy Street, 1987.

Brown, Margaret Wise. *Baby Animals*. New York: Random House, 1989.

Bunting, Eve. *Happy Birthday, Dear Duck*. New York: Clarion, 1988.

Burningham, John. *Granpa*. New York: Crown, 1985.

Burton, Virginia Lee. *Katy and the Big Snow*. Boston: Houghton Mifflin, 1974.

Carle, Eric. *Do You Want to Be My Friend?* New York: HarperCollins Children's Books, 1971.

——. *The Very Busy Spider*. New York: Philomel, 1985.

——. *The Very Hungry Caterpillar*. New York: Philomel, 1969.

Carlson, Nancy. *I Like Me!* New York: Viking, 1988.

Carlstrom, Nancy. *Jesse Bear What Will You Wear?* New York: Macmillan, 1986.

Cauley, Lorinda Bryan. *The Ugly Duckling*. San Diego: Harcourt Brace Jovanovich, 1979.

Christelow, Eileen. *Five Little Monkeys Jumping on the Bed*. New York: Clarion, 1989.

Cohen, Miriam. *When Will I Read?* New York: Greenwillow, 1977.

Crews, Donald. *Freight Train*. New York: Greenwillow, 1978.

———. *Parade*. New York: Greenwillow, 1983.

Degen, Bruce. *Jamberry*. New York: HarperCollins Children's Books, 1983.

dePaola, Tomie. *The Popcorn Book*. New York: Holiday House, 1978.

———. *Tomie dePaola's Mother Goose*. New York: Putnam, 1985.

Ehlert, Lois. *Feathers for Lunch*. San Diego: Harcourt Brace, 1990.

Emberley, Barbara. *Drummer Hoff*. New York: Simon & Schuster, 1967.

Freeman, Don. *Corduroy*. New York: Puffin, 1976.

Galdone, Paul. *The Little Red Hen*. New York: Scholastic, 1973.

———. *The Three Bears*. New York: Scholastic, 1973.

Gould, Deborah. *Aaron's Shirt*. New York: Bradbury, 1989.

Gramatky, Hardie. *Little Toot*. New York: Putnam, 1978.

Havill, Juanita. *Jamaica's Find*. Boston: Houghton Mifflin, 1986.

Henkes, Kevin. *Jessica*. New York: Greenwillow, 1989.

Hessell, Jenny. *Staying at Sam's*. New York: Lippincott, 1989.

Hill, Eric. *Where's Spot*. New York: Putnam, 1980.

Hines, Anna Grossnickle. *Daddy Makes the Best Spaghetti*. New York: Clarion, 1986.

Hughes, Shirley. *An Evening at Alfie's*. New York: Lothrop, 1985.

Hutchins, Pat. *Rosie's Walk*. New York: Macmillan, 1968.

Hyman, Trina Schart. *Little Red Riding Hood*. New York: Holiday, 1984.

———. *Sleeping Beauty*. Boston: Little, Brown, 1977.

Jarrell, Randall. *Snow White*. New York: Farrar, 1972.

Keats, Ezra Jack. *Louie*. New York: Greenwillow, 1983.

———. *Pet Show*. New York: Macmillan, 1972.

———. *The Snowy Day*. New York: Viking, 1962.

Kellogg, Steven. *A Rose for Pinkerton*. New York: Dial, 1981.

Kent, Jack. *Silly Goose*. New York: Prentice-Hall, 1983.

Kraus, Robert. *Leo the Late Bloomer*. New York: Windmill, 1971.

Lane, Megan. *Something to Crow About*. New York: Dial, 1990.

Langstaff, John. *Over in the Meadow*. New York: Harcourt, 1967.

Lester, Helen. *Tacky the Penguin*. Boston: Houghton Mifflin, 1988.

Lionni, Leo. *Frederick*. New York: Pantheon, 1966.

Littledale, Freda. *The Elves and the Shoemaker*. New York: Four Winds, 1975.

Lobel, Arnold. *Fables*. New York: Harper & Row, 1980.

———. *Frog and Toad Are Friends*. New York: Harper, 1970.

———. *Mouse Tales*. New York: Harper, 1972.

Maestro, Betsy, and Giulio Maestro. *Where Is My Friend?* New York: Crown, 1976.

Marshall, Edward. *Fox on Wheels*. New York: Dial, 1983.

Marshall, James. *George and Martha Rise and Shine*. Boston: Houghton Mifflin, 1976.

Martin, Bill, Jr. *Brown Bear, Brown Bear, What Do You See?* New York: Holt, 1967.

Mayer, Mercer. *A Boy, a Dog, and a Frog*. New York: Dial, 1967.

———. *There's a Nightmare in My Closet*. New York: Dial, 1968.

McPhail, David. *The Bear's Toothache*. Boston: Little, Brown, 1972.

———. *Something Special*. Boston: Little, Brown, 1988.

Nodset, Joan. *Who Took the Farmer's Hat*. New York: Scholastic, 1963.

Numeroff, Laura Joffe. *If You Give a Mouse a Cookie*. New York: Harper & Row, 1985.

Ormerod, Jan. *Moonlight*. New York: Puffin, 1983.

Ormerod, Jan, and David Lloyd. *The Frog Prince*. New York: Lothrop, 1990.

Ormondroyd, Edward. *Broderick*. Boston: Houghton Mifflin, 1984.

Oxenbury, Helen. *Family*. New York: Wanderer, 1981.

Pearson, Tracey. *Old MacDonald Had a Farm*. New York: Dial, 1984.

Peet, Bill. *Merle, The High Flying Squirrel*. Boston: Houghton Mifflin, 1974.

Peppe, Rodney. *The House That Jack Built*. New York: Delacorte, 1985.

Pinkwater, Daniel Manus. *The Big Orange Splot*. New York: Scholastic, 1981.

Pizer, Abigail. *It's a Perfect Day*. New York: Lippincott, 1990.

Potter, Beatrix. *The Complete Adventures of Peter Rabbit*. New York: Puffin, 1984.

Rockwell, Anne. *First Comes Spring*. New York: Crowell, 1985.

——— . *My Spring Robin*. New York: Macmillan, 1989.

Rockwell, Anne, and Harlow Rockwell. *Can I Help?* New York: Macmillan, 1982.

Schwartz, Amy. *Bea and Mr. Jones*. New York: Bradbury, 1983.

Selsam, Millicent, and Joyce Hunt. *Keep Looking!* New York: Macmillan, 1989.

Seuss, Dr. *Horton Hatches the Egg*. New York: Random House, 1940.

——— . *One Fish, Two Fish, Red Fish, Blue Fish*. New York: Random, 1960.

Sharmat, Marjorie. *I'm Terrific*. New York: Holiday, 1977.

Spier, Peter. *Noah's Ark*. New York: Doubleday, 1977.

——— . *Peter Spier's Rain*. New York: Doubleday, 1982.

Turkle, Brinton. *Deep in the Forest*. New York: Dutton, 1976.

Viorst, Judith. *The Good-Bye Book*. New York: Atheneum, 1988.

Waddell, Martin. *My Great Grandpa*. New York: G. P. Putnam's Sons, 1990.

Wagner, Karen. *Silly Fred*. New York: Macmillan, 1989.

Watson, Clyde. *Father Fox's Pennyrhymes*. New York: Scholastic, 1971.

Watson, Richard. *Tom Thumb*. San Diego: Harcourt Brace, 1989.

Yolen, Jane. *No Bath Tonight*. New York: Harper & Row, 1978.

Zolotow, Charlotte. *William's Doll*. New York: Harper & Row, 1972.

Grades 1–2

Dear Parents:

Following is a list of 97 books highly recommended for students in grades one and two. These books have been selected on the basis of their appropriateness to children's interests and represent a wide range of award-winning and frequently cited books for this age level. Plan to visit the public library or your child's school library regularly and make these suggestions part of your child's reading adventures and explorations.

Ackerman, Karen. *Song and Dance Man*. New York: Knopf, 1988.

Aliki. *Digging Up Dinosaurs*. New York: Crowell, 1988.

—— . *We Are Best Friends*. New York: Greenwillow, 1982.

Allard, Harry. *The Stupids Step Out*. Boston: Houghton Mifflin, 1974.

Asch, Frank. *Happy Birthday, Moon!* New York: Prentice Hall, 1982.

Balian, Lorna. *The Aminal*. New York: Abingdon, 1972.

Bang, Molly. *The Paper Crane*. New York: Greenwillow, 1985.

—— . *Ten, Nine, Eight*. New York: Greenwillow, 1983.

Barrett, Judi. *Animals Should Definitely Not Wear Clothing*. New York: Atheneum, 1970.

Baylor, Byrd. *I'm in Charge of Celebrations*. New York: Scribner's, 1986.

Blume, Judy. *The Pain and the Great One*. New York: Bradbury, 1984.

Bunting, Eve. *The Wednesday Surprise*. New York: Clarion, 1989.

Burningham, John. *Hey! Get Off Our Train*. New York: Crown, 1989.

Bush, John, and Korky Paul. *The Fish Who Could Wish*. Brooklyn, NY: Kane/Miller, 1991.

Carrick, Carol. *Sleep Out*. New York: Clarion, 1973.

Clement, Claude. *The Painter and the Wild Swans*. New York: Dial, 1986.

Cohen, Miriam. *See You in Second Grade*. New York: Greenwillow, 1989.

—— . *Will I Have a Friend?* New York: Macmillan, 1987.

Cooney, Barbara. *Miss Rumphius*. New York: Penguin, 1982.

Coville, Bruce, and Katherine Coville. *Sarah's Unicorn*. New York: Lippincott, 1979.

Crowe, Robert L. *Tyler Toad and the Thunder*. New York: Dutton, 1980.

Dayrell, Elphinstone. *Why the Sun and the Moon Live in the Sky*. Boston: Houghton Mifflin, 1968.

dePaola, Tomie. *Strega Nona*. New York: Prentice Hall, 1975.

Duvoisin, Roger. *Petunia*. New York: Knopf, 1950.

Fife, Dale H. *The Empty Lot*. Boston: Little, Brown, 1991.

Flora, James. *The Great Green Turkey Creek Monster*. New York: Atheneum, 1976.

Fowles, John. *Cinderella*. Boston: Little, Brown, 1976.

Fox, Mem. *Koala Lou*. San Diego: Harcourt Brace, 1989.

Galdone, Paul. *The Three Billy Goats Gruff*. New York: Clarion, 1973.

Geringer, Laura. *A Three Hat Day*. New York: Harper & Row, 1985.

Gibbons, Gail. *Department Store*. New York: Crowell, 1984.

Goble, Paul. *Death of the Iron Horse*. New York: Bradbury, 1987.

Grifalconi, Ann. *The Village of Round and Square Houses*. Boston: Little, Brown, 1986.

Hall, Donald. *Ox-Cart Man*. New York: Viking, 1979.

Henkes, Kevin. *Julius, The Baby of the World*. New York: Greenwillow, 1990.

Hest, Amy. *The Purple Coat*. New York: Four Winds, 1986.

Hewett, Joan. *Rosalie*. New York: Lothrop, Lee & Shepard, 1987.

Hines, Anna Grossnickle. *Grandma Gets Grumpy*. New York: Clarion, 1988.

———. *Sky All Around*. New York: Clarion, 1989.

Hort, Lenny. *How Many Stars in the Sky?* New York: Tambourine, 1991.

Houston, Gloria. *The Year of the Perfect Christmas Tree: An Appalachian Story*. New York: Dial, 1988.

Jeschke, Susan. *Perfect the Pig*. New York: Holt, Rinehart & Winston, 1981.

Jonas, Ann. *Round Trip*. New York: Greenwillow, 1983.

Kellogg, Steven. *The Island of the Skog*. New York: Dial, 1973.

———. *Pecos Bill*. New York: Morrow, 1986.

———. *A Rose for Pinkerton*. New York: Dial, 1981.

Levy, Elizabeth. *Nice Little Girls*. New York: Delacorte, 1978.

Lewin, Hugh. *Jafta*. Minneapolis, MN: Carolrhoda, 1983.

Lionni, Leo. *Alexander and the Wind-Up Mouse*. New York: Pantheon, 1969.

———. *Matthew's Dream*. New York: Knopf, 1991.

Lobel, Arnold. *Frog and Toad Together*. New York: Harper & Row, 1971.

——— . *Mouse Soup*. New York: Harper & Row, 1977.

——— . *On Market Street*. New York: Greenwillow, 1981.

Locker, Thomas. *The Mare on the Hill*. New York: Dial, 1985.

MacLachlan, Patricia. *Through Grandpa's Eyes*. New York: Harper & Row, 1980.

Martin, Bill, Jr., and John Archambault. *Barn Dance!* New York: Holt, 1986.

Mazer, Anne. *The Salamander Room*. New York: Knopf, 1991.

McGovern, Ann. *Stone Soup*. New York: Scholastic, 1986.

McKissack, Patricia. *Mirandy and Brother Wind*. New York: Knopf, 1988.

Miller, Alice. *Mousekin's Fables*. New York: Prentice Hall, 1982.

Monjo, F. N. *The Drinking Gourd*. New York: Harper & Row, 1970.

Numeroff, Laura Joffe. *If You Give a Mouse a Cookie*. New York: Harper & Row, 1985.

Ormondroyd, Edward. *Broderick*. Boston: Houghton Mifflin, 1984.

Parish, Peggy. *Amelia Bedelia*. New York: Harper & Row, 1963.

——— . *Amelia Bedelia's Family Album*. New York: Greenwillow, 1988.

Patterson, Francine. *Koko's Kitten*. New York: Scholastic, 1985.

Peet, Bill. *Big Bad Bruce*. Boston: Houghton Mifflin, 1977.

Pinkwater, Daniel Manus. *The Big Orange Splot*. New York: Scholastic, 1981.

Plume, Ilse. *The Bremen Town Musicians* (retold from the Brothers Grimm). New York: Doubleday, 1980.

Polacco, Patricia. *Thunder Cake*. New York: Philomel, 1990.

Potter, Beatrix. *The Complete Adventures of Peter Rabbit*. New York: Warne, 1987.

Prelutsky, Jack. *The Baby Uggs Are Hatching*. New York: Greenwillow, 1982.

——— . *Read-Aloud Rhymes for the Very Young*. New York: Knopf, 1986.

Rylant, Cynthia. *Night in the Country*. New York: Bradbury, 1986.

——— . *The Relatives Came*. New York: Bradbury, 1985.

Schwartz, Amy. *Bea and Mr. Jones*. New York: Bradbury, 1982.

Schwartz, David. *How Much Is a Million?* New York: Lothrop, 1985.

Sharmat, Marjorie. *A Big Fat Enormous Lie*. New York: Dutton, 1978.

Shute, Linda. *Momotaro, the Peach Boy*. New York: Lothrop, 1986.

Silverstein, Shel. *The Giving Tree*. New York: Harper & Row, 1964.

Snyder, Dianne. *The Boy of the Three-Year Nap*. Boston: Houghton Mifflin, 1988.

Steig, William. *Amos and Boris*. New York: Farrar, Straus & Giroux, 1971.

Steiner, Barbara. *The Whale Brother*. New York: Walker, 1988.

Stevenson, James. *Will You Please Feed Our Cat?* New York: Greenwillow, 1987.

Turkle, Brinton. *Thy Friend, Obadiah*. New York: Viking, 1969.

Van Allsburg, Chris. *Jumanji*. Boston: Houghton Mifflin, 1981.

——— . *Two Bad Ants*. Boston: Houghton Mifflin, 1988.

Viorst, Judith. *Alexander, Who Used to Be Rich Last Sunday*. New York: Atheneum, 1978.

——— . *I'll Fix Anthony*. New York: Harper & Row, 1969.

Waber, Bernard. *An Anteater Named Arthur*. Boston: Houghton Mifflin, 1967.

——— . *Lovable Lyle*. Boston: Houghton Mifflin, 1969.

Wadsworth, Olive. *Over in the Meadow: A Counting-Out Rhyme*. New York: Viking, 1985.

Weiss, Nicki. *Princess Pearl*. New York: Greenwillow, 1986.

Yolen, Jane. *Owl Moon*. New York: Philomel, 1987.

Yorinks, Arthur. *Hey, Al*. New York: Farrar, Straus & Giroux, 1986.

Zelinsky, Paul. *Rumpelstiltskin* (retold from the Brothers Grimm). New York: Dutton, 1986.

Zemach, Margot. *It Could Always Be Worse*. New York: Farrar, Straus & Giroux, 1976.

Grades 3–4

Dear Parents:

Following is a list of 99 books highly recommended for students in grades three and four. These books have been selected on the basis of their appropriateness to children's interests and represent a wide range of award-winning and frequently cited books for this age level. Plan to visit the public library or your child's school library regularly and make these suggestions part of your child's reading adventures and explorations.

Aardema, Verna. *Traveling to Tondo*. New York: Knopf, 1991.

Asch, Frank. *Pearl's Promise*. New York: Delacorte, 1984.

Babbitt, Natalie. *The Search for Delicious*. New York: Farrar, 1969.

Baum, L. Frank. *The (Wonderful) Wizard of Oz*. New York: Holt, 1983.

Blume, Judy. *The One in the Middle Is the Green Kangaroo*. New York: Dell, 1981.

——— . *Tales of a Fourth Grade Nothing*. New York: Dutton, 1972.

Brett, Jan. *Berlioz the Bear*. New York: Putnam, 1991.

Bulla, Clyde. *The Chalk Box Kid*. New York: Random House, 1987.

——— . *The Shoeshine Girl*. New York: Crowell, 1975.

Burch, Robert. *Ida Early Comes Over the Mountain*. New York: Viking, 1980.

Burnett, Frances Hodgson. *Sara Crewe*. New York: Putnam, 1981.

Byars, Betsy. *Trouble River*. New York: Viking, 1969.

Carrick, Carol. *Sleep Out*. New York: Clarion, 1973.

Carrick, Carol, and Donald Carrick. *Old Mother Witch*. New York: Clarion, 1975.

Catling, Patrick S. *The Chocolate Touch*. New York: Morrow, 1979.

Chew, Ruth. *No Such Thing as a Witch*. New York: Hastings House, 1971.

Cleary, Beverly. *Dear Mr. Henshaw*. New York: Morrow, 1983.

——— . *Ramona Forever*. New York: Morrow, 1984.

——— . *Ramona the Brave*. New York: Morrow, 1975.

Clifford, Eth. *Help! I'm a Prisoner in the Library*. Boston: Houghton Mifflin, 1979.

Clifton, Lucille. *The Lucky Stone*. New York: Delacorte, 1979.

Cole, Joanna. *The Magic School Bus at the Waterworks*. New York: Scholastic, 1986.

Cone, Molly. *Mishmash and the Big Fat Problem*. New York: Archway, 1982.

Cooney, Barbara. *Hattie and the Wild Waves*. New York: Viking, 1990.

Corcoran, Barbara. *The Long Journey*. New York: Atheneum, 1970.

Coville, Bruce. *The Monster's Ring*. New York: Pantheon, 1982.

Dahl, Roald. *Danny the Champion of the World*. New York: Knopf, 1978.

——— . *James and the Giant Peach*. New York: Knopf, 1961.

Davis, Deborah. *The Secret of the Seal*. New York: Crown, 1989.

dePaola, Tomie. *The Legend of the Indian Paintbrush*. New York: Putnam, 1988.

Donnelly, Judy. *The Titanic Lost and Found*. New York: Random House, 1987.

Erickson, Russell. *Warton and Morton*. New York: Morrow, 1976.

Farley, Walter. *The Black Stallion*. New York: Random House, 1944.

Fleischman, Paul. *The Half-a-Moon Inn*. New York: Harper & Row, 1980.

Fowles, John. *Cinderella*. Boston: Little, Brown, 1976.

Fredericks, Anthony D. *Clever Camouflagers*. Minocqua, WI: NorthWord, 1997.

——— . *Weird Walkers*. Minocqua, WI: NorthWord, 1996.

Green, Phyllis. *Wild Violets*. New York: Dell, 1980.

Greenfield, Eloise. *Nathaniel Talking*. New York: Black Butterfly Children's Books, 1988.

Greenwald, Sheila. *Rosy Cole's Great American Guilt Club*. New York: Atlantic Monthly, 1985.

Grifalconi, Ann. *The Village of Round and Square Houses*. Boston: Little, Brown, 1986.

Gwynne, Fred. *The King Who Rained*. New York: Simon & Schuster, 1970.

Haas, Irene. *The Maggie B*. New York: Atheneum, 1975.

Harding, Lee. *The Fallen Spaceman*. New York: Bantam, 1982.

Heide, Florence Parry. *The Shrinking of Treehorn*. New York: Holiday, 1971.

Himmelman, John. *Ibis: A True Whale Story*. New York: Scholastic, 1990.

Holland, Barbara. *Prisoners at the Kitchen Table*. New York: Clarion, 1979.

Hurwitz, Johanna. *Class Clown*. New York: Morrow, 1987.

——— . *Much Ado About Aldo*. New York: Morrow, 1978.

Kaye, M. M. *The Ordinary Princess*. New York: Doubleday, 1984.

Kennedy, Richard. *Inside My Feet: The Story of a Giant*. New York: Harper & Row, 1979.

Kessler, Leonard. *Old Turtle's 90 Knock-Knocks, Jokes, and Riddles*. New York: Greenwillow, 1991.

Kline, Suzy. *Orp*. New York: Putnam, 1989.

Lang, Andrew. *Aladdin*. New York: Puffin, 1983.

Levoy, Myron. *The Witch of Fourth Street*. New York: Harper & Row, 1972.

Levy, Elizabeth. *Frankenstein Moved In on the Fourth Floor*. New York: Harper & Row, 1979.

———. *Something Queer Is Going On*. New York: Dell, 1973.

Lewis, C. S. *The Lion, the Witch, and the Wardrobe*. New York: Macmillan, 1950.

Lord, Bette Bao. *In the Year of the Boar and Jackie Robinson*. New York: Harper & Row, 1984.

MacLachlan, Patricia. *Through Grandpa's Eyes*. New York: Harper & Row, 1980.

Manes, Stephen. *Be a Perfect Person in Just Three Days*. New York: Clarion, 1982.

Mayer, Mercer. *East of the Sun and West of the Moon*. New York: Four Winds, 1980.

Mazer, Norma Fox. *Mrs. Fish, Ape, and Me, The Dump Queen*. New York: Dutton, 1980.

Miles, Bernard. *Robin Hood—Prince of Outlaws*. New York: Rand McNally, 1979.

Monjo, F. N. *The Drinking Gourd*. New York: Harper & Row, 1970.

Mowat, Farley. *Owls in the Family*. Boston: Little, Brown, 1961.

Nichols, Ruth. *A Walk Out of the World*. New York: Harcourt, 1969.

O'Dell, Scott. *Sing Down the Moon*. Boston: Houghton Mifflin, 1970.

Parker, Nancy Winslow, and Joan Richards Wright. *Frogs, Toads, Lizards, and Salamanders*. New York: Greenwillow, 1990.

Peet, Bill. *The Wingdingdilly*. Boston: Houghton Mifflin, 1970.

Peterson, John. *The Littles*. New York: Scholastic, 1970.

Prelutsky, Jack. *The New Kid on the Block*. New York: Greenwillow, 1984.

———. *Nightmares: Poems to Trouble Your Sleep*. New York: Greenwillow, 1976.

Rawls, Wilson. *Where the Red Fern Grows*. New York: Doubleday, 1961.

Richler, Mordecai. *Jacob Two-Two Meets the Hooded Fang*. New York: Knopf, 1975.

Robinson, Barbara. *The Best Christmas Pageant Ever*. New York: Harper & Row, 1972.

Seldon, George. *Cricket in Times Square*. New York: Farrar, 1960.

Shreve, Susan. *Family Secrets: Five Very Important Stories*. New York: Knopf, 1979.

Silverstein, Shel. *The Giving Tree*. New York: Harper & Row, 1964.

———. *Lafcadio, the Lion Who Shot Back*. New York: Harper & Row, 1963.

———. *Where the Sidewalk Ends*. New York: Harper & Row, 1974.

Slater, Jim. *Grasshopper and the Unwise Owl*. New York: Holt, 1979.

Smith, Robert K. *Chocolate Fever*. New York: Dell, 1978.

Sobol, Donald. *Encyclopedia Brown and the Case of the Midnight Visitor*. New York: Lodestar, 1977.

Speare, Elizabeth George. *The Sign of the Beaver*. Boston: Houghton Mifflin, 1983.

Stearns, Pamela. *Into the Painted Bear Lair*. Boston: Houghton Mifflin, 1976.

Steig, William. *The Real Thief*. New York: Farrar, 1973.

———. *Sylvester and the Magic Pebble*. New York: Simon & Schuster, 1969.

Thiele, Colin. *Storm Boy*. New York: Harper & Row, 1978.

Thomas, Jane Resh. *The Comeback Dog*. New York: Clarion, 1981.

van der Meer, Ron, and Atie van der Meer. *Amazing Animal Senses*. Boston: Little, Brown, 1990.

Viorst, Judith. *If I Were in Charge of the World and Other Worries*. New York: Atheneum, 1981.

Wagner, Jane. *J. T.* New York: Dell, 1971.

Wallace, Bill. *A Dog Called Kitty*. New York: Holiday, 1980.

Weller, Frances Ward. *Riptide*. New York: Philomel, 1990.

White, E. B. *Charlotte's Web*. New York: Harper & Row, 1952.

Williams, Margery. *The Velveteen Rabbit*. New York: Knopf, 1985.

Willis, Val. *The Secret in the Matchbox*. New York: Farrar, Straus & Giroux, 1988.

Wolitzer, Hilma. *Introducing Shirley Braverman*. New York: Farrar, 1975.

Grades 5–6

Dear Parents:

Following is a list of 99 books highly recommended for students in grades five and six. These books have been selected on the basis of their appropriateness to children's interests and represent a wide range of award-winning and frequently cited books for this age level. Plan to visit the public library or your child's school library regularly and make these suggestions part of your child's reading adventures and explorations.

Alexander, Lloyd. *Westmark*. New York: Dutton, 1981.

Avi. *Captain Grey*. New York: Pantheon, 1977.

———. *Emily Upham's Revenge*. New York: Pantheon, 1978.

Babbitt, Natalie. *Tuck Everlasting*. New York: Farrar, 1975.

Baker, Olaf. *Where the Buffaloes Begin*. New York: Warne, 1981.

Banks, Lynne Reid. *The Indian in the Cupboard*. New York: Doubleday, 1981.

Baylor, Byrd. *Hawk, I'm Your Brother*. New York: Scribner's, 1976.

Beatty, Patricia. *Lupita Mañana*. New York: Morrow, 1981.

Bethancourt, T. Ernesto. *The Dog Days of Arthur Cane*. New York: Holiday, 1976.

Blos, Joan W. *A Gathering of Days: A New England Girl's Journal, 1830–32*. New York: Scribner's, 1979.

Blue, Rose. *Grandma Didn't Wave Back*. New York: Watts, 1972.

Blume, Judy. *Are You There God? It's Me, Margaret*. New York: Bradbury, 1970.

———. *Otherwise Known as Sheila the Great*. New York: Dutton, 1972.

———. *Then Again, Maybe I Won't*. New York: Bradbury, 1971.

Brink, Carol R. *The Bad Times of Irma Baumlein*. New York: Macmillan, 1972.

———. *Caddie Woodlawn*. New York: Macmillan, 1973.

Brittain, Bill. *The Wish Giver*. New York: Harper, 1983.

Byars, Betsy. *The Cybil War*. New York: Viking, 1981.

———. *The 18th Emergency*. New York: Viking, 1973.

———. *Good-Bye, Chicken Little*. New York: Harper & Row, 1979.

———. *The Midnight Fox*. New York: Viking, 1978.

Callen, Larry. *Pinch*. Boston: Little, Brown, 1976.

Cleary, Beverly. *Ramona the Brave*. New York: Morrow, 1975.

Cleaver, Vera, and Bill Cleaver. *Queen of Hearts*. New York: Lippincott, 1978.

——. *Where the Lilies Bloom*. New York: Lippincott, 1969.

Cohen, Barbara. *R, My Name Is Rosie*. New York: Lothrop, 1978.

——. *Thank You, Jackie Robinson*. New York: Lothrop, 1974.

Collier, James L., and Christopher Collier. *Jump Ship to Freedom*. New York: Delacorte, 1982.

——. *My Brother Sam Is Dead*. New York: Four Winds, 1974.

Cormier, Robert. *The Chocolate War*. New York: Dell, 1986.

Cunningham, Julia. *Burnish Me Bright*. New York: Dell, 1980.

Dahl, Roald. *Danny the Champion of the World*. New York: Knopf, 1978.

——. *The Wonderful Story of Henry Sugar and Six More*. New York: Knopf, 1977.

Duncan, Lois. *Killing Mr. Griffin*. Boston: Little, Brown, 1978.

Estes, Eleanor. *The Hundred Dresses*. New York: Harcourt, 1974.

Farley, Walter. *The Black Stallion*. New York: Random House, 1944.

Fleischman, Paul. *Path of the Pale Horse*. New York: HarperCollins Children's Books, 1983.

Fox, Paula. *One-Eyed Cat*. New York: Bradbury, 1984.

——. *Slave Dancer*. New York: Bradbury, 1973.

Fredericks, Anthony D. *Exploring the Rainforest*. Golden, CO: Fulcrum, 1996.

——. *Surprising Swimmers*. Minocqua, WI: NorthWord, 1996.

Freedman, Russell. *Lincoln: A Photobiography*. New York: Clarion, 1987.

Fritz, Jean. *Where Do You Think You're Going, Christopher Columbus?* New York: Putnam's, 1980.

George, Jean Craighead. *Julie of the Wolves*. New York: Harper & Row, 1972.

Goble, Paul. *Buffalo Woman*. New York: Bradbury, 1984.

——. *Death of the Iron Horse*. New York: Bradbury, 1987.

Graeber, Charlotte. *Grey Cloud*. New York: Four Winds, 1979.

Highwater, Jamake. *Journey to the Sky*. New York: Crowell, 1978.

Holm, Anne. *North to Freedom*. New York: Harcourt, 1974.

Holman, Felice. *Slake's Limbo*. New York: Scribner, 1984.

Hopkins, Lee Bennett. *Mama*. New York: Knopf, 1977.

Hunter, Mollie. *A Stranger Came Ashore*. New York: Harper & Row, 1975.

Konigsburg, E. L. *From the Mixed-Up Files of Mrs. Basil E. Frankweiler*. New York: Atheneum, 1967.

Lee, Robert C. *It's a Mile from Here to Glory*. Boston: Little, Brown, 1972.

LeGuin, Ursula K. *Catwings*. New York: Watts, 1988.

L'Engle, Madeleine. *A Swiftly Tilting Planet*. New York: Farrar, Straus & Giroux, 1978.

London, Jack. *The Call of the Wild*. New York: Penguin, 1981.

Lowry, Lois. *Anastasia Krupnik*. Boston: Houghton Mifflin, 1979.

——— . *Number the Stars*. Boston: Houghton Mifflin, 1989.

Magorian, Michelle. *Good Night, Mr. Tom*. New York: Harper & Row, 1981.

Maruki, Toshi. *Hiroshima No Pika*. New York: Lothrop, Lee & Shepard, 1982.

Mayer, Franklyn. *Me and Caleb*. New York: Scholastic, 1982.

Mazer, Harry. *Cave Under the City*. New York: Crowell, 1986.

——— . *Snow-Bound*. New York: Delacorte, 1973.

Mazer, Norma Fox. *After the Rain*. New York: Morrow, 1987.

McKissack, Patricia. *Mirandy and Brother Wind*. New York: Knopf, 1988.

Mowat, Farley. *Owls in the Family*. Boston: Little, Brown, 1961.

Murphy, Jim. *Death Run*. New York: Clarion, 1982.

Myers, Walter Dean. *Scorpions*. New York: Harper & Row, 1988.

Newman, Robert. *The Case of the Baker Street Irregular*. New York: Atheneum, 1978.

O'Dell, Scott. *Sarah Bishop*. New York: Houghton Mifflin, 1980.

——— . *Sing Down the Moon*. Boston: Houghton Mifflin, 1970.

Paterson, Katherine. *The Great Gilly Hopkins*. New York: Crowell, 1978.

Paulsen, Gary. *Hatchet*. New York: Bradbury, 1987.

Peck, Robert. *A Day No Pigs Would Die*. New York: Knopf, 1972.

Raskin, Ellen. *The Westing Game*. New York: Dutton, 1978.

Rodgers, Mary. *Freaky Friday*. New York: Harper & Row, 1972.

Salassi, Otto. *And Nobody Knew They Were There*. New York: Greenwillow, 1984.

Sargent, Sarah. *Weird Henry Berg*. New York: Crown, 1980.

Schwartz, Alvin. *Scary Stories to Tell in the Dark*. New York: Harper & Row, 1983.

Sebestyen, Ouida. *Words by Heart*. New York: Bantam, 1981.

Seidler, Tor. *Terpin*. New York: Farrar, Straus & Giroux, 1982.

Shreve, Susan. *Family Secrets: Five Very Important Stories*. New York: Knopf, 1979.

Silverstein, Shel. *A Light in the Attic*. New York: Harper & Row, 1981.

Singer, Isaac B. *Zlateh the Goat and Other Stories*. New York: Harper & Row, 1966.

Sleator, William. *Among the Dolls*. New York: Dutton, 1975.

Slote, Alfred. *Hang Tough, Paul Mather*. New York: Lippincott, 1973.

——— . *The Trading Game*. New York: Lippincott, 1990.

Smith, Doris. *A Taste of Blackberries*. New York: Crowell, 1973.

Speare, Elizabeth George. *The Sign of the Beaver*. Boston: Houghton Mifflin, 1983.

Sperry, Armstrong. *Call It Courage*. New York: Macmillan, 1971.

Stoltz, Mary. *Cider Days*. New York: Harper & Row, 1978.

Taylor, Mildred. *Roll of Thunder, Hear My Cry*. New York: Dial, 1976.

Taylor, Theodore. *The Cay*. New York: Doubleday, 1969.

Uchida, Yoshiko. *Journey to Topaz*. New York: Scribner, 1971.

Voigt, Cynthia. *Dicey's Song*. New York: Atheneum, 1982.

Wallace, Barbara. *Peppermints in the Parlor*. New York: Atheneum, 1980.

Yep, Lawrence. *Child of the Owl*. New York: Harper & Row, 1977.

——— . *Dragonwings*. New York: Harper & Row, 1975.

Index

About the Author

Anthony D. Fredericks

Tony's background includes extensive experience as a classroom teacher, curriculum coordinator, staff developer, author, professional storyteller, and university specialist in children's literature, language arts, and science education. In addition, Tony visits hundreds of schools and communities throughout North America working with educators, librarians, and children on effective literature-based learning strategies.

Tony has written more than 30 teacher resource books in a variety of areas, including the celebrated *Social Studies Through Children's Literature* (Teacher Ideas Press), the acclaimed *The Complete Guide to Thematic Units: Creating the Integrated Curriculum* (Christopher-Gordon), and the best-selling *The Complete Guide to Science Fairs* (Scott, Foresman) which he co-authored with Isaac Asimov.

Not only is Tony an advocate for the integration of children's literature throughout the lives of elementary children, he is also the author of such award-winning children's books as *Weird Walkers* (NorthWord), *Surprising Swimmers* (NorthWord), *Exploring the Rainforest* (Fulcrum), and *Clever Camouflagers* (NorthWord). He is currently a professor of education at York College in York, Pennsylvania, where he teaches methods courses in elementary education. Additionally, he conducts many national and international storytelling/writing workshops for teachers, librarians, and children each year.